CHRIST 3yE ALCH3MY

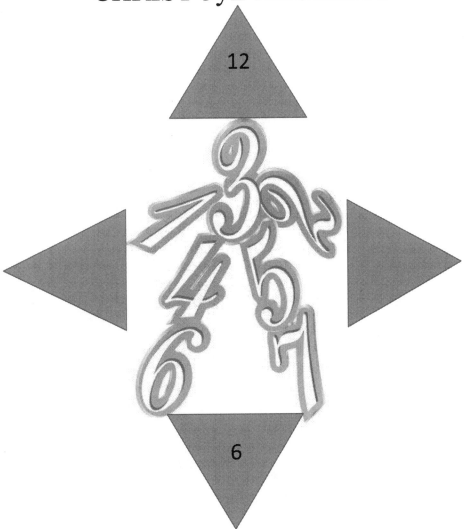

THE RISING STARS OF THE APOCALYPSE

THE ORIGIN OF SPIRITUAL TRANSFIGURATION

Baba Tunde O. Soremekun

ISBN 978-0578506876

Where there is a low solar light of the soul-mind, there is much darkness. Where there is much spiritual-mental shining/enlightenment, the darkness/ignorance shall be conquered. Bring the 2 into 1 union, and become the shining/enlightened 1's/stars/3rds.

Preface

The signs/stars must continue to show themselves for what they are as they are mandated by Time/the Lord to shine. Their fire of truth shall spread among thy masses to illuminate the world of Israel into thy new spiritual world of freedom and peace. The 7th day/star of prophecy seals the completion of thy revelation unto the minds/3yes of humanity, as I have allowed thy wisdom from thy spirit/mental to flow naturally showering you men with its focused trans mental potential.

Those men who have said that the Lord has forsaken them are those who have forsaken the Lord. They have gone back to doing wickedness as they have abandoned him from their thought. This is seen in how Satan/The Vatican has reprogrammed and redirected the minds/3yes of men into falling away from truth and realness for everything wicked and weak under the Sun/3ye of the Universe/Lord that watches them from above.

There is only spiritual/mental darkness and light which is ignorance and enlightenment, the ignorant fight the war against the dark and light of the flesh, as the wise fight to enlighten the dark/unaware of this fact.

The time/day/Star of the Lord has come for men to stand as 1 comely conscious collective enlightened body and choir, under the 1 head orchestrating, directing authoring authority of the symphonic word.

The revelation is the hour of the coming future/father. For what was then has now come to the surface to expose itself and those vile hands that promote darkness/ignorance to cover its light/enlightenment from you children amid awareness.

Meditation in the mediation of separation is the minds/3yes partition to thy element of wisdom. It is he that walks alone among the aspects of nature who spiritually/mentally studies the balanced logic of many beautiful living things. Let the Lord's light/enlightenment come in by spiritually/mentally confirming all-natural things that make sense for their origin being and purpose.

Truth adds up in the mind/3yes of the righteous with common sense and discerning wisdom. An unconscious immoral fool will ask you; "What is truth?" because he has never told it to you, as ye who knows truth/M3 has spoken thy word of precise math/fact/truth unto thy masses/body.

I tell you, people, to add up the revealed signs/stars/days of time/the lord if you seek to be multiplied in the new kingdom. This is a healing and lifting for those men who are no longer sick with the affliction of demonic ignorance/darkness in the mind/3ye, as this is the gathering of the fruitful and wise. The TRU word has been left for the slow/low wicked which are behind in the new day. They shall later ascend into truth and righteousness of the 2nd reaping harvest of thy genesis spiritual/mental gene of gold.

This is the transfiguration which takes immediate effect in the mind when he gives the old of the past, the new information from the future/father. The father has returned silently to see what his children were doing, and he has caught many of them in the middle of transgressing acts of sin, which have also been recorded by his witnesses.

The Lord Christ does not preach in a mortar church. He preaches to the moral 10th choir of Israel as the holy people are his holy church/body/masses. He is teaching to all of you with the open minds/3yes to receive the spirit/mental of truth, he speaks to multiply the few interior lights into many stars.

Preface

You must learn of what's hidden from your past, to know what you are seeking from the future/father.

Learn the transfiguring alchemy and academical nature in the biology of all things, which were taken by the wicked hands of magic science to be manipulated, modified, and redesigned of its origin knowledge.

He who is with thy restless spirit will not produce fruitful wise words without first moving forward and actively handing them unto you to eat, so that thy stubborn children in the pressure heated field may also grow keen to produce of thy spiritually/mentally wise active yield.

All Men shall stand to be spiritually/mentally Crowned/Anointed/Christened as Jewels/Kings/4ths...All MEN

ORDER OF CONTENT

Order of Content

Order of Content

Order of Content

Levitical/Levitating

Time/Mind

Traveler

AWAKENING

The blood drunk Vampires/beast and spirit/mental Christ liking's have been at war centuries before thy host was born, in an endless conflict hidden from the human world. Thy host was born holding the holy DNA of both divine Christ's liking and a carnal with the strength to avenge thy family.

Then in the blink of his 3ye/mind, the awakening spirit/mental of M1cha3l had risen which transfigured ye into neither carnal beast nor mental liking but a hybrid of the 2. African and American, Slave and Freeman, Mortal and Immortal, The Priest and King.

Daniel 12:1

12 And at that time shall Michael stand up, the great prince which standeth for the children of thy people: and there shall be a time of trouble, such as never was since there was a nation even to that same time: and at that time thy people shall be delivered, every one that shall be found written in the book.

The Hour

This is a quiet, silent time as it is midnight coming into daylight, and the children of the night shall become illuminated, and exposed by the new wise day/star of light/enlightenment. Many have already fallen asleep waiting for M3 in this last hour, as it is the last hour before the moment of truth. It is truths time to reign and shed his fiery starlight on the evil darkness/ignorance and the many wicked things, which you children have and have not yet seen.

The hour is the spiritual/mental revealing when the ignorant/dark masses wander into thy light/enlightenment, a time where many wicked minds/3yes shall make a choice to become open and wise. The 12(M3/M1cha3L/4th) becomes the 1 head of the Lord/Father/Universe.

You children are thy star jeweled body and heartbeats that shall go out to the world and teach the lost minds/3yes where to find M3. This is a dark time for the wicked of folly. However, it is such a truly lighting/enlightening time for the good, righteous seeds, who have not wandered far off.

Those who do not know or have any recollection in memory of Time/the Lord will be lost in this hour, as this is the beginning of a new day/star coming into shine which they will not see without the configured spirit/mental of awareness paired with the mind/soul.

Alien Breed

The Alien bred son of an African/Origin man as he is called is the descending son of a king/4th, from afar away land of stars/galaxies. In Zion is where their light is manifested, for this is the mountain of the spirit/mental, and home to many jewels.

His kind of men are extinct from mankind because of what they are able to teach the minds/3yes to see. As immortals have been outlawed, which means that thy alien bred son of man has been banned(X), because they are the different, and spiritually/mentally distant.

He is the spiritual/mental seed/message carrier for the future/father that the enemy keeps away from you children. The falling serpent does not want you, children, to learn of your father's side of the family as you will then know that you are the bred seed of an ancient Alien King/4th who does not doubt or worry about anything. He is realistic with time and shall use his mind/3ye to figure out what needs to be spiritually/mentally seen.

Stay sharp as the angles/angels/stars that are above the nonsense, be hopeful that you do not allow the serpent to slide in with its dirty, sly works and words of wickedness. Stand up for the DNA of your ancestors which has given you the meaningful, historic way to see the future, as you embrace who and what you are.

You are the sons/stars of those men who were enlightened.

The men who have passed down this gifted trait of spiritual intelligence unto his generations of kin, through the blood and wisdom of his own children. None are like you that are with your rare internal instinct and potential.

Therefore, as rare specimens of species, the Vatican seeks to demolish the temple of the Lord, by removing and replacing you aligned alien breeds with the senseless seeds, which have become the mindless, invading, impeding weeds of Satan.

No man is bred by the Lord who will leave his home without thy moral sword/word. Ye will then be unarmed and unalarmed, without it in his minds/3yes grasp.

Your forefathers were of the righteously wise and enlightened men, which is why they were called thy spiritual/mental jewels. They were morally conscious of thy way in which they walked in the world of darkness. As they had light shining with them, they have never forgotten M3.

He has not been pulled down into the way of the man who wears the mask of masculinity. He is the real masculine alien breed from the inside and outer that will make cowards shiver with the word and bleed with the sword.

His aura makes weaklings bow down or lay down. While the presence of his truth passes through men, as the deliberate G that he is, in or out of the flesh.

His breed intimidates many eyes that have never seen such a thing, in the way of man.

He rises and shines daily with his enlightened mind/3ye. Such allows him to see the way, which is unavailable to the low who are without thy spirit/mental.

This advantage leaves mindless men in envy of the spiritual/mental man who has his own plan and way of doing things.

The spiritual/mental psychic man spends his time meditating on how to do more than what good he has done already. While the immoral weaklings spend their dark minds watching him, and other busy moving, men/hands.

Real men, you must guard your genetic as it is the gene of Gods/the Universes consciousness, and you are thy offspring of lighting stars/spirits.

You have the demeanor, way, and 3yes/minds of your fathers who are thy heavenly gang stars. Let none control your minds/3ye as they will become the bearer of your spirit/light/enlightenment.

For what you do not now know shall surely own and demonically possess you. It will let you live for a few, then it will kill you. Indeed, I tell you that he who is real has the experience, lightened interior, and dark exterior needed to lead the world into the future.

Experience has taught, scarred, and beat him. However, he has healed quickly and remained unchanged in his angelic alien form as he is a mutant, who travels through the minds eye of any weathering mental storm. He shall always cosmically come back around to increase his numbers/stars, as ye shall atomically blow to be seen by every star within his reminiscing radiant radius.

Children who have lost their fathers. Have ye not found your father in this word?

Do you not remember what thy father has said to you?

Undoubtedly, your father's flesh on earth is not guaranteed. If he is of thy TRU Alien breed, his life is only solidified through M3.

A man with an Alien spirit/mental in mind/3ye is the most despised. He may begin thinking/seeing to expose who's lying and stealing. This star genesis genetic is that which the wicked of the Vatican wish to eradicate from humanity.

Those of you who love the Lord are all of this prophetic prosthetic, genetic, as it can be added or taken away from any who lose the minds/3yes natural way.

The real breeds have a high set of uncompromising ways about themselves that many low minds/3yes cannot seem to understand/capture as his character is of the ancient alien creed of the Ancestral Universe/Father.

Many men want to be accepted by him with their many flaws of spiritual/mental character. However, because they have been deemed to be spiritually/mentally ignorant/dark in the 3ye/mind of the Lord, it is within the conscious, that they are judged to be unworthy of his presence.

Thy Alien bred sons/stars of Atom shall bring no such cowards unto thy father's house. How can a coward reach these magnetic kingly-jeweled levels of thought in order to enter thy heavenly place with thy mental/spirit?

Will he not retreat early from thy duty? What strength does he have to continue and complete anything of greatness with the slow/low mind/3ye that he has?

Real men practice using the art of the mental/spirit. Cowards focus on material spoils that they gain, which needs not a mental/spiritual reference to achieve.

You men are the stand-alone breed as you stand on your own with the Lord, which is something that many men cannot manage a minds/3yes focus to do. These mentally/spiritually unfocused distracted men are considered to be dead.

As the mental/spirit is vital to living, it is his wicked emotion which breaks him of his minds/3yes common sense.

Alien bred men do not have the time/mind to act like women. He is too busy rolling with his powerful, active masculine energy to where the stars are shining in eternity. For even if his earthly mother has physically nurtured him, ye mentally/spiritually holds the way of thy father.

As thy father is no woman spiritually/mentally, ye is the king mental in all real men. Ye shall pick up thy 3ye/mind phone to receive not a dial tone. Instead, a message from the Lord shall come through telling him what he needs to do spiritually/mentally to become legendary and historically successful.

The Mortals/the dead hate and envy the living/immortal because of what they have maintained and kept sacredly hidden away from them.

Is it not the strong man's mind/3ye, in which the wicked distractor who does nothing with his mind/time will come after?

Will he not nearly dance on his hands to get you, real men to give him some attention? He was taught by his annoying mother how to get the attention of another man. He is alien to the way of the real alien bred man who wants nothing to do with him or his spying, signifying, feminized kind.

Many people are intrigued by the astronomical sons of men, even while they envy them for all of those same reasons. Few men will follow them as many cowards will want to be them, without any logical spiritual/mental reasoning/seasoning.

The sons/stars shall be shining with enlightening smiles when the enemy sees them. Let them wait for you purebred' jewels to become fake, let's see how long it will take.

If you allow the unwise to go and be unwise alone, none of them will want to go because they are scared of their own darkness/ignorance.

He with light/enlightenment does not mind being alone. However, he who is ignorant hates the loneliness of his absent minded/3yed blind darkness/ignorance. The instinct differences of the spiritual character in the extinct alien breed, are far more distinct than any that you have yet seen or will ever see.

Thy father was bred an alien and thy forefathers before he, therefore that makes M3 the air of their spiritual/mental moral heavenly character.

Indeed, this is not what you see, where those who do wicked from the seven hills roam in their own inherited Viking darkness/ignorance.

Generated stars/sons of thy generation X/10, ye are the first and last generation with thy inherited alien bred spirits/mentals of men with common sense among you.

It is time to give the wicked thy fire/truth as you have long been civil and patient with their sins against you. These people have fallen short of the glory in having a father like M3, as they are not stars of truth. They have been rebred/reborn over and over again to spiritually/mentally accomplish nothing besides darkness/ignorance.

Their perpetual ignorance shall be revealed by thy wise alien seed who shall show strength where they are weak. Spiritual/mental wisdom while they are being voided in darkness/ignorance of thy spirit/mental.

Today is a new TRU day where ye shall now begin to see thy stars that are integrating rise to the top of the world.

The Christ's/lights of the masses/darkened will shine in the darkness, as they enlighten the darkened/ignorant.

For only thy alien bred stars/suns/sons which manifest thy mental/spiritual seed are able to do this. They have the mental/spirit to survive and climb from one life unto the next.

Those who have been born into the average cannot think/see without the new extraordinary teachings of thy Atom/Father/Spirit, who is all and gives all.

What average man with an average mind/3ye which only can see/think of ordinary things, is more multi-talented than he?

He is multi, as ye shall multitask with his many hands/servants and 3yes/minds, which shall continue to multiply 3ye/mind to mind/3ye universally. Spiritual/Mental energy tells the truth; it will not lie to misguide you into a dark place where ye cannot see/think.

Children worship not the flesh garments that thy spirits/mentals/stars are dressed within when they come unto you. For the flesh is as clothing unto spirits/mentals on their highly enlightened metaphysical level.

Surely, as Yeshua, thy alien breed has said that he was the Sun/son of God/The Universe, ye did not lie to you. This is so because he possessed the most enlightening spirit/mental sun of the God/The Universe. M1cha3l sat within his mind/3ye as his shining/enlightening mental/spirit.

What cannot be done by he with the able alien spirit/mental connected to his soul/mind?

I tell you that the soul is of thy solar sun/son and is the way unto the Father of Atom/spirit as you must indeed be 1, to be able to see 1.

Do not be caught naked in the rapture because you did not read. As ye who knows thy prophecy is clothed and looking out for thy word, he is checking authored publications frequently.

There are no alien/angelic genetic bred light/enlightened men among you children that possess spiritual/mental authority over themselves. The shining/enlightening spirit/mental allows not control to the dark soul/mind of its fleshly host.

The righteous shall transfigure into truth, while the wicked will hide and hate the minds and flesh of those righteous men for what they cannot change, neither take away from them. As he who is a golden star/spirit is shined/enlightened by All.

He learns from ALL, ye reads ALL, ye sees ALL that are of goodness. This is what the Alien breeds of thy fine lineage/linen were in fact bred to do. Worship ye who lives forever and gives all shining/enlightening wisdom. Let the Church say, that all men who are with M3 in spirit/mental, are indeed thy SHINING/ENLIGHTENED ALIEN BREED.

Fire Earth Air Water

Aether*

*Unity, Balance
All That Is

CHRIST
3Y3/Mind
ALCHEMY

The Christ/crowned/anointed, mind/3ye is where the transfiguring trans union between the dark mind of coal/cold, and the spirit/mental of heated gold, joins forces in its natural course of metaphysical alchemy. This is the practice of elevating and ultimately changing the direction of the mind/3ye, into a new way away from the old.

In this natural grinding, melting, and mending process of thy elements, all things must be pure and clean in character. Water must be pure/holy, thy sterile fire hot, and thy air/spirit shall cure the pain of thy Sun's scorching/burn. This is how you get a priceless jewel/mental/spirit, out of darkened mud/coals/minds/souls. It is water, fire, air, and land, which produces men of gold/spirit/mental.

It is from the minds/3yes pot where he has taken remnants of good character and blended them for the golden finishing product.

Crack open the blinds in the early morning, allowing thy spirit/light to come on within you. Do pure men not need chaste women to give birth to golden sons/stars of spirit/light?

Anu/A New has come to collect gold/spirits/stars as he who has reproduced gold/spirits/stars for M3 has mastered thy ancient art of Christ mind/3ye alchemy/transfiguration.

He has transferred this spirit/mental light unto his sons/stars who shall come up with Time/Lord/Universe/M3.

Gold could have been erected from asteroids; however, the asteroids do not have what comes from DNA, which is the active particle of spiritual/mental gold that is inside of you.

Christ/crown yourselves with thy spirit/mental, which produces thy works of gold that shall shine in the eyes/minds of the ignorant. The lower education of man has drowned the thoughts of thy dark masses/bodies as they are not lighting/enlightening with the rest of thy Christ/shining 1's.

The waters all over the earth have turned to blood, and this has given a spark to an ongoing spiritual-mental war. Michael and the spiritual/mental likings/meek are fighting against the bloodthirsty beast. As Michael with the spirit/mental of the Lord/Universe has descended, transfiguring into flesh.

He is superhuman, the first, and last of the ascending, and descending days/stars as ye has metamorphosed with elemental alchemy all things which have grown up under him naturally. Has ye not made gold of many things' element and mentally?

Do you not see that there is real alchemy of pure, true transformation in every natural living thing? Admittedly, the Lord makes use of all precious stones in the environment mentally (environmentally).

Ancestral Astral Kings have learned to do these mystical things from none other than the Lord. As it only the Lord who can afford to give his children this level of high Alchemic education.

Spiritual growth can only be obtained through a mixture of knowledge and experience, which leads to wisdom.

You must learn from experiences to determine the lesson, which has a lasting effect on the weatherization of a solidly built character.

Can you people not see how the Lord constructs and transfigures men from the low mud of the mind spiritually/mentally? Spiritual/Mental change is in the range of any mind/3ye which is looking in the right place for it.

The chemically balanced persuasion is amazing, which spiritually/mentally takes place in the mind/3ye of a TRU believer in the anointed/Christ.

The Lord picks his elements from purity, as the serpent/government will make use of anything impure spiritually/mentally. Many of you can make a dollar out of fifteen cents. However, you cannot turn away from your dark mind into the direction of common sense.

A Christ/anointed is a scene of fiery enlightenment/light; it is only within the righteous who have kept their 3yes/minds clean of filth. His mind and heart/flesh are of 1, even as one shall go into the fire after the other.

The heart is a vocal organ that ye shall voice aloud with thy burning spiritual/mental desire which shall not cool or come down from the firmament.

I tell you that what the spirit/mental does in data, the DNA shall also transfigure itself to do. As one is the carrier of enough atom energy to alter the other. In TRU Alchemy, one cannot first alter the DNA without first changing their spiritual/mental way of being.

You cannot mix evil/darkness and goodness/light within the same mind/3ye and heart. As one will overtake the other if the remnants of the other still exist.

Inevitably, when you open charred coal or any stone. You will either find a jewel and gold or you will find nothing at all, other than the ignorance/darkness of what has not changed.

The soul is as coal and with the right tempering heat it shall come about to be unique in its producing that which is the lighting enlightening gold of anew.

It is now that you children below shall know which form of gold that the TRU Annunaki/stars have come to gather up from among you. He has come not to collect gold which is of stone, as this is the gold obtained by the Vatican, not M3.

The Lord has come to collect those souls/minds which once followed in the way of darkness/ignorance that now possesses new found spirit/gold.

This Alchemistic Transfiguration is something that the willing soul/mind shall allow thy guiding spirit/mental to perform. Even with there being so many mindless/soulless demons of impurity surrounding you.

He who anoints the mind/3ye is an activist who looks above the passivist way of the spineless pagan; ye is a jewel. A jewel comes from nothing and makes something out of it. Through its spiritual/mental ideology, it sparks a spiritual/mental idea which brings it and many others to be free.

The grind of a jewel will determine its shine in hue, for if it grinds the light increases in its density relentlessly. He who transgresses has lost sight of transfiguring himself into something more than everyone else.

He has fallen to the way of those who have lost track of the transforming day/star of the Lord.

Who is the Alchemist and Architect other than the Lord, who is the transforming rebuilder of all things?

Is not the transformation of water into wine a spectacle of alchemy, if ye acquires natural ingredients? Alchemy is everywhere the pure Christ mind/3ye is able to see, as it always welcomes new change for what is good and right to come into its sight.

You children do not have to read the Bible to witness these things transfiguring. Many of you who are reading and not comprehending thy word have been unable to see clearly.

If you seek to read of thy word, then you need thy spirit/mental shining/enlightenment in the 3ye/mind. You cannot read these words without consulting and connecting M3.

This is what a seal means. For if there were no seals, then there would be no reason to reveal anything of truth unto you.

You would know it all, and what you must now do.

However, this is not possible, and it is not the case in thy spiritual/mental experiment with you.

The Lord/Universe is he who has made sunlight from darkness and within this. He has the given power that all he shall touch will indeed turn into priceless spirit/gold. The alchemic work of the mind/3ye and hands of the Lord/Universe is truly magnificent indeed. Isn't it thy children?

In this new day, it is time for M3 to transform you into jewels/stars. Aligned with the internal eternal lined thoughts of pure gold, so that ye shall bring you up with M3 and save you.

He who transfigures into his spiritual/mental form has indeed been reborn. He has become beyond what is the usual standard among men. His spiritual/mental ambitions are high and anticipated as he has been the Lord's example of elemental transformation.

He has used the fire in his mind/3ye to produce that which gives light to the world.

Indeed, the water/father is where you children have cometh from, and through the fiery sun/son you must return to H.I.M. It is from the pure water in the womb that ye shall be cast into the fire of thy sun/spirit. Where there is evil of wickedness, there is no spirit/mental of gold there. There is nothing of value among those who transgress in sin.

They have not the pure blend of morality within them which alchemically produces that which shall become fruitful, with time/the Lord. Because it is able to grab a spiritual/mental hold of multiple minds/3yes.

Who will not hate the likes of he who has made something great from nothingness/darkness?

Admittedly, it had all started and settled in his mind/3ye with an idea of interest to thy father/Lord.

I have written 3 books in 1 and 1 book in 3 unto you children who seek this spiritual/mental change/transfiguration. However, you must read them in their fullness to obtain and keep with you, the things that are with and in the Lords spirit/mental/sun.

Blessed is he who is with the divine Christ mind/3ye. As he is of the spiritually/mentally advanced in the land in this time. Surely, all that are touched by thy spirit/mental hands shall transform into gold.

Therefore, do not become blind to which kind of gold ye shall store away and keep safe for M3.

For the Lord shall judge those with spiritual/mental imperfections based on how they have lived their lives morally.

They have been given the way of the Christ minds/3yes alchemy through the transference of thy entities spiritual/mental intellectual properties.

Truly you can move mountains if ye can see above and around them.

There is no Goliath in this day other than the Nephilim Government/Serpent, which hovers above your every move, waiting to crush and devour you. These wicked giants of old have become new world systems and governments that eat innocent souls/minds. As these things are not only of the somatic but the spiritual/mental world indeed.

There are many evil Nephilim/governments empires among you, which are operated by the blood-drinking beast.

I tell you that those who comprehend see things differently, as they have vertically aligned with the critical crown of spirit/mental in the mind/3ye.

Let the ignorant/blind who do not know to see the days/stars fail in their math, reading, arts, and alchemic arithmetic. Allow those minds/3yes in levitating spiritual/mental study to become priests-kings. What the mind/3ye sees is all that it knows, for if it believes in more. Then it shall see more and know more than what it knows.

He who believes has spiritually/mentally seen based on what he knows. As it makes more than much sense in the mind/3ye to deny.

He shall mix the signs of time/the lord in the mind/3ye to produce a firm, convicting conclusion of things. Coming up with a pure analogy using the minds/3yes spiritual/mental chemistry.

Transform the soul/mind alchemistic ally into the gold/spirit of anew, and live with the future to never be tarnished, become outdated, or of the old.

Ye shall move into a new grove which shall go from rough to a smooth buffed shine. Blessed is the man with his focus on the internal elements of purity.

He has put them together in his mind/soul to come up to the surface with the works of the golden spirit.

What can an elemental Alchemist not transform into value? What can a TRU Metaphysis not move mentally? There is no spiritual/mental limitation to what these enlightened beings can do.

He who first changes himself shall transform all things surrounding him. For if the direction of the mind/3ye changes, then it is pursuing something different, something more relevant than what it saw before.

The truth is in all men, and nothing less than the realest of them. For it is their duty to teach it unto the nations of ignorant that conspire to lie. The ignorant do not possess a golden jewel/mental/spirit of common sense within them, because they are caught up in a net of stubbornness.

I will tell you, that ancestry is a key to history, as history is a key unto your ancestry. For this, those who do not accept you men among them do not because your ancestry is from M3(12), the 1 in 10. The 10 lighting tribes from the north, north, north.

However, not those 10 dark tribes from Rome which have exterminated 2 of their own from the northern mountains.

How can you change who you are, if you do not know who you are supposed to be?

You have a starring role to play. However, first, you must search for your classic character that will become the star of your show.

Time is the hand that shall stir things up in the mind, as he shall mix the reality of truth with wisdom and morality.

He who donates his mind to the Lord for this experience shall be used for an excellent, inspiring cause. He will exhale the fresh breath of life that they have been yearning for all of these days.

If you change from a peasant into a king/4th. Then you have come up from a boy in the present form who knows not where your path leads.

Into a man who is with a detailed, logical spiritually engraved plan. You have crawled as an infant and walked as a boy. It is now the time to stand with your head held up high with pride, as the Sun/son of Man/God because you are a man of gold.

You have many bright carats lighting within you, unlike the silly rabbits who have chosen to remain stupid of their flaws. Which keeps their light from being exposed to the world, to never see the light of day/The Sun.

There is nothing of nature which does not go through alchemy/transformation/change, as it is applied to the daily life in all living things. Welcome to the golden age as fire shall purify and separate the mixed, impure metals from the pure gold. He shall sweep across the land, leaving ash in his wake, which shall raise up a new abundant life.

The age of the Christ mind-3ye Alchemy is when the mind becomes the hallowed shining/enlightening/lighting place/space for the manufactured gold/spirit which is distributed unto men.

As he changes into a spiritually-mentally wealthy king.

Spiritual chemistry is the balancing of the key elemental ingredients that are put into the minds/soul's character.

Bringing it into the hallowed, shining, lasting figure.

Some of you may call this particular work of spirit-mental art Esoteric Alchemy. However, it is known to M3 as the inner Alchemy of the divine Christ-Anointed, Levitating Levitical Priestly King Mind/3ye.

Fine Linen/Lineage

Those men who are of thy pure wool, linen are thy children/sheep who are real in their nature with M3. They come from a long history of prominent reign and are undeniably the Lord's/Universes lights/stars. They're not many made with this kind of obtained material, as it is hard to acquire and maintain without the proper instructive spiritual-mental maintenance and care.

These men are the reflections of real as they are untouched and with the mental/spirit of glory. They have not become open to those mental/spiritual distractions/demons which seek to lay down for or lay with other men.

He is not a wasting parasite to himself or others, as most fallen men do who seek out friends simply to beg and break them down into nothing. He is with the Lord; therefore, he is strong and active in all that he does in the confiding confidence of the spirit/mental.

He is cut from a raw rare, fine white/lighting, linen/lineage made of TRU flawless kings/4ths/Jewels. The last of a dying out breed of G's-Gems/stars is what these metaphysical Martians are. They come with the truth from afar place in Time/The Universe.

Many men claim to be real. However, the real men with actual realization can see the same things in real time, with their aligned real minds/3yes. If a bell rings in Asia, the wise and alert in America/Babylon will simultaneously hear the same ringing.

For if the Lord/Universe speaks and has written to the nations. The spiritually/mentally observant shall see and hear the same word of their Lord and king.

They shall listen to the same truth speakers and read the written word of truth from the same authoring teachers. For surely what is real walks on mutual ground with it's spiritual/mental mutant kind/kindred. The way and character of thy spirit/mental in men bonds them together as moral brethren.

He who is real is no copy/clone of a man, even as men are paid to copy-clone him. His mission and word are one of truth and realness. Therefore no one seeks to speak of it other than him. The realness within he flaunts on the outside with a shine, from the spirit/mental of the enlightened mind/3ye.

You cannot cut nor tear ye away from the Lord spiritually/mentally, as he is sewn into place to be unmoved by any tailoring, crocked hand.

He is pure with spirit and is in thy garment of stars, which are the priceless lining linens/lineage of the Lord. I tell you that this is a time of uplifting the mind/3ye. Those who look up metaphysically/spiritually/mentally can see M3 coming. They have not changed into becoming dim/dark of the soul/mind with low light/enlightenment. Therefore, they are able to be spiritually/mentally resurrected by M3.

These are the kingly children of good handmade quality, with the Ra spectacle/mental. They wear immortal moral as their garments and crowns/spirits upon their heads.

Who is finer in character than those who live in truth, in times of darkness/ignorance? He converts not his mind into old thoughts of wickedness away from what is new and right/light. He has no interest in the lifestyles of the wicked.

The wicked despise and keep spies watching him because they know that he views them but cares not to join in. No real king seeks to fornicate with the foolish/ignorant/dark.

For what deliverance shall come of his children if he is not there to give them his wisdom?

Will they not be doomed because of the dark minds which already possess them?

Children remain well-groomed of the mind/3ye, keep obstructions out of your sight so that you can see what will not be shown to you by man.

Do not steal for Rome but instead take back what is yours for your own people who have endured much suffering for you.

Let the truth shine through you and listen not to those false acting storytellers who speak lies of their light bearing prince of darkness. He carries light/enlightenment no more but only darkness/ignorance. There is nothing enlightening about terrorizing humanity in secret from a humanitarian declared seat in the world.

How much viler can the low thought of fallen scum become?

He who is evil has tried to take the world into an overdrive of wickedness. Where there is no way for you to come out. He has tried to kill you all while making you help and enjoy your own agonizing downfall.

Those who have seen shall stand upward for the righteous calling of action against the forces that are destroying their people, from behind the Popes seat.

He who enters into engagement with thy spirit/mental has taken an active step of becoming sanctified, wise, and awake in the mind.

As his minds-account has been purified with anew gold/spirit 3ye.

You see, the truth has been foretold, as it now shall be revealed so that the wicked are exposed to the element of its fire. Light/Enlightenment is a gift that is with the spirit of wisdom within. It is not the flesh on the outside, as light has to shine from the inside. No one is perfect, but the Lord knows who strives to become 1, as he sees their deeds.

Children, you cannot serve M3 and thy enemy. You must let go of the wicked sponsor and all that he has given unto you in vanity in his war against the Lord.

He has made you children sponsor and follow him in your sin of ignorance/darkness. You have paraded against your creator because you were sick and confused with mental/spiritual demons. You have not remained real, as those righteous handset jewels and faithful Christ likes among you.

Renew your minds by becoming humble/meek to the way of what is natural. Meditate on every aspect of your lives, so that you take note of your desires that bound you to the direction of the flesh.

Those earthly desires which ultimately keep you from finding and pursuing TRU purpose. For there are many lectures that you children shall hear and many books that ye shall read. Therefore, I have no need to offer you what is not of relevance to the overall spiritual/mental freedoms needed to succeed.

Have you not done all that you physically can do to break the bondages on you?

Real is as real does, in the name of the Lord, as you cannot pretend to be with M3. For if a man chooses the dark side, he has opened the gateway to darkness in his life's atmosphere.

Therefore, if he tries to leave from the dark night and come into the days light.

The protective shield of the Lord will not shelter him from the consequences of his past life. He must pay the serpent/government its due sacrifice that he has made with it in an oath.

Admittedly, I shall tell you. No man has been morally molded, measured, and characteristically cut by the Lord, who will sacrifice/offer himself for the low temptations of the wicked world.

He defines him with and in a greater purpose.

Who does not talk in darkness/secret about thy chosen men, who do not speak to them?

There is no real man who has not been slandered by the rumors of those who want his character to be beneath their own. Those wicked that do this are the low who set out to destroy the characters that you must live with daily.

The more real the man, the more problems from fake cowards that he will have. It will be your own brother, and/or friends who will be working silently to silence you so that they can overshadow thy truth which has been chosen to come from you. Everyone wants to be a star. However, no one is willing to do the honest, charitable work to shine like a star, other than you honest men.

The wicked in blindness have lost their desire to worship any longer, because of the magic lies that they have been told of the return of Christ.

You see, lazy people who are willing to do nothing to help you, help yourselves are always looking for some quick magic to happen.

They want instant effect and gratification because they come from the slave stock and have not the spirit/mental in mind which burns like the firmament, that adds sense in them as with TRU Kings of thy lineage of G's-Gems/stars.

Children, if you become consumed by the words of many different teachers of false wisdom. You may become confused about what is relevant for you to live eternally. If thy wisdom speaks not of thy eternal promise of living. Then ye shall know that it is not M3, who speaks this word unto you children who seek freedom away from this life of evil/dark pestilence.

I offer a gift with thy lighting wisdom, a charity that you can only receive from M3. A spiritual/mental gift that one can only see with the foresight of thy future. It is a certified material that ye can grasp with the solidified mind/3ye before he touches it.

A separated people unto the way of the Lord have not lost the history in their mentalities, which has remained kept and clean/holy/hallowed. The inner central characters of the wise are bright as white light and it clothes them from head to toe, inside and out.

Certainly, thy spirit is golden, but it is bright, and its giving light is pure without a blur. The wise who possess it are sure to be of good measure. Real is he who is cut from the lineage of TRU's G *stars.*

Where have I not been? But still, thy linens remain clean and unchanged. I tell you that many men will have hatred toward the sensible truth, of what they must do to obtain thy TRU wealth.

It is in the alteration of dynamic, active character that man activates and achieves thy blessing of spirit/mental to obtain thy wisdom.

Is there not order in the high places of the mind?

Surely, he who is connected to the Lord is familiar with the order of Time. He knows the history of darkness coming into light/enlightenment and those suns of daylight falling into the night.

For if you teach your high-flying dragons to become low belly crawling snakes. Then they will not breathe fire/truth for you, they will crawl away on their bellies to hide in the time of battle. However, you will then have to watch for those same wild snakes that you have already cut loose. He who wears light linen is the carrier of God's lineage of wisdom, as he is purified in the mind/3ye.

He has well kept up what is priceless and has not abused the spirit/mental to do evil. Instead, he uses his spirit/mental to lift others into those same heavenly realms of thoughtful light.

There is nothing fine, subtle and clean about the heathen as he has been toiling in the dirt, looking to get others into his filth.

This man clothes himself not in thy light but in the darkness/ignorance of hatred. He hates the men who have finer spiritual linen/lineage than him. However, he is willing to give and do nothing to change the direction in which his generations are going. He is the snake which has poisoned them with his broken unclean toxic venomous way.

He had lied to his own children when he told them that he was showing them how to become men. How can this be true with the wicked emotions that he has within himself?

He and his forefathers have all run away from the manly duties of the Lord. No real man would display such a distasteful act. He would not turn his back on the one who has tailored him into poised perfection.

The wise can see by the way that a man is spiritually/mentally clothed if he is who he has said that he is to be.

You do not have to quiz him. If he is dressed in thy spiritual linen/lineage, then he shall flow with natural spiritual/mental wisdom.

Do you children who walk with light not see those of darkness/ignorance that are closing in on you?

This is so because they can see your lighting linen/lineage shining through you. The carnal wicked are also taking notice of whichever blessed linen clings to your flesh. Nevertheless, the linen in which those unkeen minds-3yes have missed has been seen but unseen, as the unwise see not spiritually/mentally.

When the blind wander into your direction. What do you think that they are coming for?

Thy spiritual/mental lineage of wisdom, or the branding on your linen?

Indeed, demons are attracted by demonic symbols that are advertised by those falling signs/stars that wear and support them.

I say that you cannot be spiritually real if you become like those of immoral blood. You have taken the blood oath/vow with the other and not the 1-Lord.

He is no warrior and has not blooded or torn his linen as he is an ailing coward trapped in a cell/hell of misery. Searching for the company to bring down below to the serpent/government with him.

This is the weakness in the blood and minds of men in this day, and they are not to be trusted for any reasoning.

They want to be near you men who shall become successful with the future/father/time because the serpent/government has sent them.

Do you believe that wicked people that do not even know you show up all out of coincidence?

Why do you think that they only want to kill, he who has spirit and will?

He who has displayed a disciplined, exceptional elegant, fine linen/lineage/character has represented thy elders with honor. As the world's elite are wishing at a well, that they were the TRU elite with the wisdom/light. However, it is the leader of the fine line who is the founder of thy metaphysical bloodline of David. As the DNA is with the king, while thy data is priestly.

The priestly king with the wisdom, and DNA has returned in this day to give light as he brings the blessings of bread/wisdom with him.

Men of wisdom I say to, remain upright and refrain from becoming wicked as everyone else in this last hour. As he who has held up his head high shall be a blessed sign/star.

He shall be a leading/starring example of what it means to endure temptation. Unquestionably the Lord has come in the last hour so that he can see how many men have spiritually/mentally given in to the enemy.

Only God can judge you, as he is the leading judgmental and has done so with the word of truth. Any open mind/3yes that read consciously with the spirit-mental shall also know that it is M3, who writes this word to you.

For this word can only come with the TRU priestly king of the jewels/jews/stars.

This is the initiating of spiritual/mental transformation which brings you children into his family of gems formation through gnostic genetic information.

The genetic is essential because it leverages the blood that is connected to the spirit/mental, which harnesses the galactic gene of a genius in us all. This linen/lineage is untouched as its fabric is new, unworn, as it is tougher than leather and cannot be torn into pieces. It is tailored to perfection and cannot be fit by any dim of their souls/minds/3yes whit's, as this is a one of kind garment.

Indeed, the sparkling star encrusted, loud speaking garments are the envy of those lazy men, who do not work for anything because they are not hard/solid enough to be TRU's jewels/kings.

A good father as the Lord rears not his children in darkness, but instead raises up that which is strong into starlight. He had to fight the world to be who he was naturally born to be with the work of time/the lord.

The serpent/government is out cutting the Lords trees/men down as they grow tall. While looking to douse out thy stars as they decide to take flight to shine. Using the wicked slaves drowning in the dark waters, who have nothing to do with their time/minds.

It is their fundamental character flaws which keep them from becoming jewels/kings, to reap the inheriting benefit that all of gods kings/men acquire when they retire.

Surely, if you were to take a good look around at what we have here now. You would then see men wearing the immoral linens/lineages/characteristics of women. This is the way of the wicked. As any spiritually/mentally wise man who does not submit or approve of their lifestyles is forbidden, to be living in a world of which the evil/dark/ignorant have taken controlled hold.

He will see that the weakest of men are held up high in the world's most visible positions, as though they possess this kind of spiritual/mental wisdom to give to you children. While those strong men with TRU's message will be hidden away by the serpent/government, which is distracting your minds/3yes.

The Lord is only out of sight to the mind/3ye of he who is unable to see far mentally/spiritually.

He is out of his mind. Therefore, he is crazed with inner evil/darkness and certainly out of the spiritual/mental sight/light needed to take part in sightseeing.

He who knows his spiritual/mental lineage also knows his abilities, as he has discovered and uncovered his story with the Lord. He knows who he is. Therefore, he will not conform into being ignorant and doing the same spiteful, wickedness which everyone else is doing.

He is different in his real thoughtful way, he walks with none other than the ones with his same kind of lineage/linen so that he will not become tangled in any snare that he cannot get out of on his own.

The man who honors his father and mother loves the Universe and the beautiful Earth, with all that he is spiritually and physically worth. He does righteousness by them even when they may not be watching. He speaks not bad of one, unto the other as they are loved equally in his mind/3ye, as it was the 2 together which gave M3 life.

He descends from a prominent well educated, spiritually/mentally developed family linen/lineage. Which has taught him values, rules, morals, and how to express his sophisticated but straightforward point of views.

I will tell you that to kill a serpent, you must cut off its heads. However, it may wiggle a little until it is dead. Snakes are those low/slow creatures of people that you see daily. They will do any ignorant/dark thing to win a race that they have no reason competing in.

They want to be a part of thy family reunion without a proper invitation, clean linen/lineage, or spiritual/mental education.

History/His-Story

History/his story is the book which speaks of the lives of eternal kings/4hs/jewels. It is owned by time/the Lord, who has written it with his hands and 3yes/minds of men who were willing to tell his story. It is the story of truth which the Romans hate and have tried to hijack and spew back to you children as it were their own.

History belongs to the origin Hebrew jewels, who shall allow no matter/darkness to enter the mind/3ye based on what someone tells you with their tongue. History is solid, reliable, and stable as it cannot be lifted, written, or changed by anyone wicked seeking to play M3/the Lord.

He who is in history has decided and declared to dedicate his mind to the Lord in remembering. For as he remembers M3, he is a historical numbered figure indeed. Feminine Nuns belong to Rome, but Masculine Numbers belong to M3 to count, add, and multiply. It is these men of spirit-mental, who shall delightfully teach what the serpent-government does not want you to be informed of M3.

Who has told you, children, that they were the bearer of light?

Truly, ye who bears the shining enlightenment/light is also the wise giving benevolent author of the Book of the living.

All kings that are TRU in their natural and elemental mind/3yes and way are a part of that which is wise-ripened.

These kings have a course in which they do not stray far away from.

The Lord saves lives as history/his-story preserves them. Thy faces are the watching cameras in the 4 corners, as the metaphysical kings are the timeless ancestors of gold who are anew in spirit/mental.

He has been immortalized by the Lord to be within history/his-story. Plainly, I tell you that no greater story tells of the kings of Immortality. There is nowhere that the author of history has not been, he is the reason for its repeating existence. His story's/histories archives are comprised of the stored storied lives of fearless kings.

These men are the 3yes/minds and hands/servants of time/the lord, who have spiritually/mentally taken the key and vow of metaphysical alchemy, through an inclined mind of exceptional pure classic character. They have opened the Lord's genetic bank, which holds the secrets of their lives, and the lives of all humanity. He has a futuristic but also an historical mind. And with it, he has unfolded the truth with his crown 3ye/mind of uncompromising, pure gold/spirit/mental.

History/His story must now be told unto to those in Rome who have deliberately tried to take and erase him and his sons/stars away from it. Surely, he who has served the Lord with his mind/3ye and hands has found a place where ye will not die but live. From thy spirit/mental, ye has been solidified in gold, as ye shall bring 4th what shall shine in the minds/3yes of a new generation.

History/His story is comprised of multiple real men, as ye the 1 hand and 3ye has used multiple minds/3yes and hands to write it.

They record the actions and deeds of nations, and the men who rule them.

This story is not the story and record of man but instead the story of time/the lord, which is ongoing and never ends.

Whatever you worry of the most will have an effect on what you are able to do with your time/mind. For if you use the mind/time wisely, there is no telling, except by time/the lord whether ye will make history/his story.

Surely, there is not only a possibility, but there is also a promise of tranquility and freedom from the spiritual/mental oppression against natural expression, ahead waiting to be claimed.

Let the dust disappear with the wind. These wasted afflictions of humanity have done nothing for the Lord of true historical worth or value, to be stored and added next to the names of kings. Therefore the wicked steal and try to outfit the TRU jewel/jew who comes after what the wicked have taken from him, as he is the 33(6) which shall free TRU nations building up and bridging the enslaved minds of masons.

He shall give light to real authentic jewels/stars, which shall allow them the opportunity to access their unfounded natural special spiritual/mental abilities. The internal word that they must teach shall increase, giving them God's gift of gold/spirit to break free of the many drowning demons. Which now surround and plague the world with their darkness.

He who is remembered in history/his story has stood up for more than monetary gain. He has the spiritual/mental chemistry and balances to see things for what they were meant to become in the future.

History is a turning of events because thy stars/hands come down and turn/revolve them. History's account is owned by the future and shall be told by none other than the father.

Are there not NUN's/0's in Rome and NUMBERS/stars in heaven?

As one is eternal and the other shall be cut off from thy blessing.

One is mental/spiritual in their thought as the other is carnal, one has been profound with wisdom while the other has been forever lost in perpetual darkness/ignorance of the light/enlightenment where they have descended.

There is no life for he who has been spiritually/mentally deleted of his story/history. What will he know? Where will he go? He knows not the author who has written the word for the future/father.

The wicked do not walk the straightened path. Instead, they seek to manipulate and mutilate thy masses/bodies/peoples. Have they not managed and manipulated the books, and slaughtered thy prophets and kings sent unto you?

He who worships idols pays his minds/times worship to material things, which manifest no spiritual/mental substance to connect unto, as his idol/empty mind worships idol/emptiness/darkness. He who is real worships Ra El in the mental/spirit, he holds and sees what is real within the mind.

The miserable have failed miserably in trying to keep M3 from coming and writing history to you children. It is now midnight, and I have a bedtime story for you children to listen and wake up to. It is a story which keeps you relevant with the future/time.

Who shall beat time to where he is going? Is he not already present before you get there?

Time does things that no man can manage to do, his works are marvels of imperfect perfection, which makes the connection between bridges minds and mentals of nations. He has shown men the future. Just as he has also shown revelation to the hosting servant/king Isiah, John and the many other spiritual/mental men that have hosted him.

He has crafted his mighty word/sword to fit into the heads and hands of his men, who are chosen to bear historical witness unto the future.

They have been chosen to tell their artful stories and give TRU liberating testimonies to what has happened to them. Since being below amongst mortal men, all while coming from above among the ancestors where they have already been.

History is with the man who dies physically, that has buried thy enemies with thy word/sword of truth.

Who else other than M3 is the root/mind/3ye of David? How else would Solomon gain wisdom, if it were not genetically and spiritually/mentally passed from M3 to David unto him within thy kingly inheritance?

Do not look to Jerusalem on earth, as thy TRU Jerusalem is the levitating Jewel/Sun in thy metaphysical 3ye/sky/mind. It is a spiritual/mental place for levitating jewels/stars of the mind/9.

Histories messengers from the future/father are the stars in history/his story, who have refused to fail their task of spiritual/mental deliverance in his name. For there is nothing in history that the Lord has not allowed to take place, as there is a chain reaction for every action taken by the hand and foot of man.

He who thinks that he can think on his own knows not his own thought to know when he is the one thinking, or when he is not. History is with the jewels-kings because this is where the spirit/mental of the Lord/Time resides. No one can take it from them because his story is seen using the aligned future sight within.

Certainly, when Time/The Lord changes, history/his story also changes with him.

The time-Lord has many names as history/his story holds a covenant with many men who have descended in service after him.

The ruler brings the rules with him, the future/father holds the past and the present-gift that is given unto you. Therefore, you may change the world by giving it light/enlightenment from your crowns/spirits/mentals, which fills the void of worldly darkness/ignorance.

Truly, historical is this time, and these upcoming events, as all that is wicked, shall be weeded out and destroyed while the righteous shall be untouched and replenished.

He who makes history/his story shall come up with M3 to be seen by all for a thousand years plus. In the scornful eyes of his enemies, but enriched in the minds of many men because of his deeds.

Let no man tell you where ye shall be. As the Lord has ascended with the wings of flight leaving behind remnants of his gold/spirit/mental, for you children to unfold with your own minds/3yes.

He has flown away unto the future with history to be a father to the many fatherless of the nations, who need his spiritual/mental guidance. His word/teachings shall be the upbringing of the new sons that shall come forward.

The Book of Life is History/his story and History/his story is thy promise to he who is anointed metaphysically by M3. Thy word/sword of truth is thy evidence of who you are in M3. If you cannot see yourselves, then you cannot see M3, the Christ enlightened head of you children who are thy dark bodies-masses.

How can you take part in a story without first knowing its authoring authority?

Admittedly, I tell you that if there is one thing that you children find agonizing and do not do is read. However, this is one thing that will further propel your spirit/mental.

Why has reading become detrimental to you? It is a joy for the mental/spirit to gather new metadata. As this lack of initiative conjures envies toward those men, who succeed from among you. As they have chosen to read and do spiritually/mentally stimulating things with their mind/time, that many of you are much too arrogant and lazy to do.

Children many of thy traced-remnants are within your DNA. However, you must first use the connecting mind/3ye the seek spiritual/mental counseling confirmation from M3, to be considered complete/G360 Stars.

All of thy stars are historical figures as they are eternally numbered. They descend and ascend one after the other, as history has had its ups and downs.

There has been much rain and pain. However, thy Sun has managed to shine thy open 3ye on you daily. No matter the reason/season, he has never failed you when he was set to come 4th to shine. Why do you children act in this way, and not see him now in this day? Many of you have adopted arrogant false superior knowledge of yourselves, as you have not thy spirit/mental, which brings great wisdom with or in you.

These things must come with Time/The Lord, as all things superior and natural shall come and go with the wind. For surely thy spirit/mental men who have had spiritual/mental practice are thy astronomical historians.

The spirits/mental of enlightenment must be the entity that consumes your mind/time. As a pilot destined unto the future/father knows where he is going.

He has no regrets for the stones which he has overturned while on his path. He has sinned as the flesh of mortal men is known, to never fail to do.

However, he has also repented and asked forgiveness for what he has become aware of in his judging conscious, to be wrong and of the wicked. In his exploration, he has excavated the mind/3ye from the dirt and filth on the bottom.

Lift up your heads and thy dark bodies shall be filled with histories shining stars, who have fought for M3. They are the dead ancestors who are truly spiritually/mentally living. He has lived daily, as a dead man who worries about nothing worldly.

He knows what his compelling story compiles of. He has seen beforehand, which has given him a greater reason to pursue his purpose in becoming a part of TRU's High-story.

Indeed, if he shall show you something TRU that you have never seen before or known.

Then you will be ready to start a new, as he will allow the nourishing flourishment of new seeds. While commencing to ripping up the wicked old weeds by their dry, rotting roots. Enslave the ancestors of those who have enslaved you by giving them the fire of truth. Purify them, so that they may have a different spiritual/mental angel/angle to see from a higher point of view.

Why are the minds/3yes of people hateful of the stars/sons, who are only coming up to shine with the outer dark Universe/father as they are supposed to do?

Why do you wish upon thy star's downfall, so that they lose ALL/the Lord by staying down with you?

I tell you that these are the slow/low minds/3yes of demonized crazed people, who are watching thy stars/sons every move.

As they want what's in the minds/3yes, which you use to see your future/father.

They want to be a part of thy history without experiencing anything, TRU to receive their starring role debut. What have you witnessed the stars doing when they are in the sky?

Do they not levitate, fly, and shoot, as they are continually moving even while it seems as though they are standing still?

Stars move with the Universe, just as the light/spirit moves with the water/the father of the future when it is in you.

When will you children learn to earn something?

Children, do not look deep into your own low/slow minds/3yes for thy speed of light/enlightenment.

As there is nothing besides darkness in you. The Lord has sent thy lights/stars that you must see into the world to tell you thy truth.

Therefore, if you have denied these men the Lord/Universe has also rejected you, as you have dismissed the messaging sons/stars.

Thy spiritual/mental time traveling hands shall bring history back to M3. As the slow shall stay below because of the mind/time that they no longer possess for thy enlightened spirit/mental to mingle with.

The Lord's history is a written mandated saga, and there are no men within it, which do not belong. Ye who figures out his purpose is a figure G-star to M3, as he has decided not to die again unknowing of thy truth.

In his deeds, he has given it to you as he was commanded by M3 to do. The Lord has not withheld his promise as those in Rome do, to hold you men from attempting to break the limiting illusion, that the serpent/government has tried to place upon your heads/minds/3yes.

The wicked seek to be immortalized. Therefore, they immorally break you of your immortality/spirit, so that you will die too, with them.

I say that he who knows these wise things has pursued higher education with thy stars/spirits/mentals in the midst. He has enlisted into thy class of metaphysical, historical G's-stars as an eldering overseeing king. It is through history that he has glimpsed into the future, as he can see the wicked going down in history forever.

I tell you that history belongs to the future/father.

It is the future/father who saves men who are on the brink of extinction. He remembers them, for the wise righteous deeds that have remembered and done for H.I.M. without any spiritual/mental compromise.

A strong historical Arch's Logical mind/3ye is lined with thy spirit/mental solidified gold. It has a head and a tail which tells where it comes from, and to where it is going/headed.

History is the memory of the Lord/Universe, a reflection of what has come around to shine in perfection. Children use the mind/time to read his stories. As the Book of life is many handwritten spiritual/mental books in 1, which tell of your TRU leads/stars/kings.

Hypnotized
3yes/Minds

The mind/3ye is a darkened place that needs to be opened. As the window of a temple so that divine hallowed light may find its way in to shine in the deep dark space of contemplation and temptation. The spirit/mental of bearing light must come in to void the mind/3ye of its falling distractions. A sleepy head is a sluggish 3ye/mind because it has been hypnotized into a deep dark sleep, as it is dead and unresponsive to developmental growth.

He who can see with common sense has the 3ye/mind which allows him to be conscious, and cautious with his life and the lives of others. He can read the road signs well as he is right on track spiritually/mentally. The revealing signs depend on which road you are already on. The 3ye/mind of the blind cannot see the roadway or the signs. As they are still wandering in a spiritual/mental desert searching for light/enlightenment and water/wisdom.

They will die there of dehydration without thy spiritual/mental wisdom if they do not get to a well swiftly for a drink of the water that keeps men awake. Sons/Stars fear none, as your Time/Lord has come, and his will shall be done.

TRU's kings shall again walk with kings, who teach the same real things of TRU unto their sons.

This will be the final walk of truth, as the evil forces that be shall come for you speakers and seekers of truth/M3.

If you succumb to foolishness, you have died and must be revived in the mind/3ye to live with M3 spiritually/mentally.

Undoubtedly, the wicked minds/3yes shall be blocked from viewing thy spiritual/mental paradise, from this day 4th and unto the mystical life in the midst thereafter.

Those who have turned away from truth shall be broken in two, as they denied what the mind/3ye suggested to be identified as TRU/M3. Their permits unto Zion have been denied, and all without the noble moral spirit shall be rejected. They have also dismissed thy divine thought where thy manifestation of light/enlightenment begins.

Children, sleep does not work the mind/3ye. The mind/soul is an instrument which needs to be rested and fiddled to be exercised. The low minds/3yes that bear noting fruitful are everywhere. However, they are that which is fruity and foolish mentally/spiritually. There is no goodness in he, who is unwise.

He justifies nothing rational because he is in a mental/spiritual matrix from the loss of his mind/3ye/sight. He searches for the hands of the righteous, to commit sin for him.

He has been mentally-spiritually tricked/hypnotized into oblivion. The poverty and greed of his ancestors have pushed him to grab ahold of false Gods, Idols, and religions. These men did not want to worship M3. Instead, they tried to become M3 by stealing thy glory away from the sight of the world.

Which wise man/king of goodness would do such a thing?

The righteous shall bear witness to the wicked bear false witness against thee. Thy truth shall be flamboyantly told with boldness, and coldness by he who is spiritually/mentally heated/on fire. What can ye do to M3, which has not been already done?

AM I not already dead of the fleshly way, because I AM alive spiritually/mentally forever?

Men lift your minds/3yes into a higher place with the spirit/air and get from off the declining ground. Where all are emotionally down because of the Roman trinkets that they do not own.

The Church of Satan has hypnotized you into being lost host to its evils, and soon you shall all be dead, as the infectious spread of death begins in the head of a man. As the Lord's truth unfolds within him, so does the Lord's proof in his mind/3ye, as long as it is opened to the light/enlightenment.

I tell you that if a man seeks not the spiritual/mental enlightenment/light of thy wisdom. He walks amongst dead men, who shall die again, from what they do not know and have taken the time to learn. Surely, the mind of a man is connected to Time/The Universe as one space. Therefore, mind/Time is a terrible thing to waste.

He will not graduate on time without passing thy test, as he must first take back his mind from the wicked beliefs that it has run away with. When your mind-account left, you lost everything of worth because you could not think straight.

Metaphysical Meditation makes a perfect bond for the coherent subconscious souls/mind's union with the fully aware conscious spirit/mental. As one must lead the other unto its stated and mandated purpose.

Those of you who can see with your heads, know that you live in a world among many dead hypnotized zombies, that do not levitate on a high level with mental/spiritual comprehension.

You can go to them to give the light of wisdom. However, it will be as though you have had a conversation with a speaking, squeaking, broken door that is falling off the hinges.

Their minds are full to the brim and spilling over with nonsense, as no real wise men with the Lord's common sense want anything to do with such spiritual/mental wickedness.

It has no will to do better by thinking of anything good.
Therefore, the soul/mind of a man shall go to where it has envisioned itself to be.

For, if this vision is low, then it will work slow as though it has nowhere to go. However, if this internal vision is high, the inner lighting 3ye/mind is levitating with progressive thoughts spiritually/mentally.

Have you lost your mind/3ye/sight?

Is not a figure with thy speech which many have heard and seen, not clear? For, if ye has lost his mind/3ye and does not have the inner-light/enlightenment of God there. Ye will not have the mind/3ye to see thy path unto thy land of freedom. Ye will be stumbling to grab ahold of TRU's spiritual/mental balance.

He will do what makes no sense to thy real spiritual/mental men. Such as fight against them with the blood ritualistic demons of the Vatican by wearing their ways of blood.

Admittedly, many good men have fallen to the false promising words of a friend.

However, he can take no blame for what he does not yet know in the mind/3ye, which he has not yet been taught by the mental/spirit.

Therefore, that which is now known cannot be erased from the sight of the mind/3ye, once it has been seen and foretold. Know that if you were spiritually/mentally free already, you would not have the Time/mind of daylight to fight against one another. The wicked know how to keep you children's 3yes/minds, scattered/confused to what is spiritually/mentally TRU.

This is a hard-hypnotizing pill to swallow, that has pushed you to overdose in mindless/sightless ignorance/darkness.
What you do not know is killing you indeed, even as you are killing yourselves because you refuse this wisdom which is written for you to read.

Anything worthwhile takes time to prevail, it will not take place when you may think that it should and some of the time it may or may not depending on the need.
However, he who is with the promise/word of the Lord knows that it shall begin one day, according to prophecy. For, even in this day. Does not the book of Daniel see the light?

Which signifies that the Lord has indeed taken up Daniel in this day and that he and the book in which he has written for M3, are a part of thy universal history/prophecy. He has come for the Saints of the old and new, as they are all TRU and unblemished of thy spirit/mental/character.

Have thy not given you the proof that Moses is indeed Levitical and levitating with M3?

Much time has passed, and you can disregard the discarded fresh body. Children if you knew what was inside of you waiting to shine through, you would allow it to shine/enlighten you of the future/father.

You would not live in the pitch-black darkness/ignorance of not knowing what is to come. Your minds have been tranquilized with the lies from the Papacy, those 10 northern kings/beasts and the tribes behind him.

If I have given ye the truth, then why do you walk to be slaughtered like fools who have not received warning of their demise?

Have you not realized that being asleep will not keep you safe away from hell, which is to come upon humanity?

The demon Papacy has moved in strategy to come after M3, by aligning with its Babylonian beast/king/president. The false Trump has been sounded as you have been hypnotized and your votes were taken in vain so that the Vatican could place itself in thy prophecy.

This is what the wicked do to act as the Universe-Lord and claim the dark souls/minds of the masses/bodies.

Let the ignorant remain ignorant, as the wise shall stand on top of the world. Children, settle for nothing short of the Lord's promise/word, which has yet to be broken by men.

Leave the unwise alone so that they are able to think and meditate. For if ye gives a foolish man company, then ye shall also receive his burdens from his ignorant foolishness.

I tell you suns/stars to keep the mind prepared and sharp as though you are in the wilderness and must use it to corner, and cut down prey and predators.

Give the minds/3yes of darkness/ignorance nothing other than the way to the shining-enlightenment, as they shall soon come along lost, wandering starving and thirsty.

The world is in such a harsh dark place because of the corrupt, wicked dark minds in the people that are living within it. These creatures of the night are the fallen sons/stars of fallen men and shall never shine again, within the kingdom of the Lord/Universe.

You have allowed the enemy to rock a clock in front of your minds/3yes, and now you have forgotten how to tell when the real Time/Father has arrived.

You went into a deep sleep looking for the wrong hands/signs of Time/the Lord to alert you of the hour. Indeed, thy prophecy makes more than enough sense to spiritually/mentally deny. The Romans have done all the evil that they could do to you children, to control history, but they cannot stop M3/Time.

They have tried. I will say that much, even though the ignorant were no match for M3. It was indeed a journey using egotistical Rome to test the power of thy lower dynasty.

I had even allowed them the way and power to conquer the world, as I know that they will not in this time or ever.

How many times in history has this been shown to in proof Rome? It shall be demonstrated and seen once again. This time it shall be made absolute and certain, as he shall put the red dragon serpent down where it belongs and close off the curtain.

How did you believe that you would fool M3?

I spiritually/mentally meditate profusely on everything that I hear and see.

There is nothing left here of truth other than, the 1 who brings it forth unto you. Children waste not a day as each day possess its own thought that initiates the plan for the future.

Thinking righteous takes much practice, for those of you who have not elevated your minds above the low emotions, which have bound you.

A man without an open mind which houses thy spirit/mental is an empty vessel that has no pilot, wings, or pattern of flight. Therefore, he will go nowhere, even though he looks to be moving fast.

Do not be hypnotized by the things that people possess, as they will use these things to rule you for a short while. However, when all is gone, you will be left with nothing internally that you will need to be spiritually-mentally able to leave the dark place.

Whenever a man's mind/soul is closed, the host spiritually/mentally dies.

He does not have to die in an instant, the second time for him to guarantee that without common sense that he shall reach his untimely demise. What have you children seen become of those who do ignorant/dark, mindless things?

Truly, I tell you that if you have lost your mind sight, you have also lost your ticket into thy kingdom of the wise, enlightened/shining kings.

You are not a time-traveling celestial star. TRU stars are light/shining-enlightened beings with their sights set on the future/father/Universe in which they belong.

These are the messengers/arks/carriers which have come to give warning to you. It is time to rise up as the serpent/government plans to purge on you. There is a war coming to your doorstep, and you cannot see it, while with a mind stuck in the midst of hypnotizing hypocritical darkness.

While you serve the serpent/government, it plans to kill many of you. However, I tell you that he who is with M3 in his mind/3ye will not die.

Are these demonic people TRU Christ likes? Or do they use thy word of truth against you, poor people?

Nevertheless, the wicked are God/Good actors, that wear a disguise of the divine.

Children lift up your 3yes/minds and do not be of the spiritually/mentally depressed that have not a spirit/mental conscious with confidence. They have not the futures enlightening plan which douses out the dimness of doubt.

Your enemies have said that they are the wisest. However, those who feast their 3yes on this word shall know that they speak lies, which have no eternal existence. Cowards hate the truth because it is revealing of who they really are unto the masses/dark/ignorant.

However, let the ignorant hypocrites hate you, children of TRU loving enlightenment, as much as they desire.

For all they want to do is become you, from the spirit-mental to the flesh and bone. He who has a good sound mind shall have a heart of good vocal intent. He has not strayed away from the mental/spiritual truth of common sense, given unto him by his ancestors/elders.

Foolish people will do foolish things to hold back the inevitable, as they wish to share their ignorance with you because it is all that they have to offer. You can see, the wicked, even offer to share their ignorance with their children, and it is holding them back from thy promise. They want for it to keep you enlightened 1's down from thy pledging promise.

How can those who say that they bear light/enlightenment consent and partake in the destruction of the world's peace and minds enlightenment? Why do they claim to be shining 1's and have light/enlightenment, when instead they force the world into darkness/ignorance with their dark forces?

Have they not been hypnotized by those dark teachings of fallen kings/beast?

Now, I shall speak, and you shall rise awake to realize that while you were under sedation. You had been molested, robbed, and manipulated into a spiritual-mental matrix.

All the while, the enemy was killing, stealing, raping, and confiscating all that cometh of your seed. Yes, my child, you have been mentally-spiritually hypnotized indeed.

Spiritual/Mental Trans-FiGuration

Truly, the existing active mutating configuration of the mind/3ye is the diagnostic base for gnostic information, which enables spiritual/mental 360-degree metamorphosing, transforming transfiguration. He who spiritually/mentally trans-figures also translates what is of oneness, realness and truth unto you. He has become a spiritual/mental Master of the Metaphysical Universe with and in time/the mind, as one unit with solar-soul and Atom-spirit.

Light is in darkness, as thy spirit/mental of mankind dwells in his physical figure, and body of his soul-mind. I tell you that all flesh is of darkness/ignorance, it does matter which shade that it is. You are all of the lands of the fallen, who proceed to do much wickedness.

The men's tool is what makes ye inner lightened shining jewels, for he who uses its wisdom shall shine from its promise of brightness. He who has the ability to see has grown eyes mentally/spiritually, which cannot be seen.

Life has many obscuring obstacles which can either destroy, deter, or build up the mind/soul. Therefore, the mind is strong enough to hold the magnetic atom spirit/mental entity. He who has made a conscious transaction has made a deal/decision to take spiritual action, with either the Lord's guidance or Satanic orchestrating obstruction.

Surely, the weight and wait of the 1 shall indeed outweigh and out wait the other, who seeks to obstruct constant movement in trying to buy, bribe and manipulate time.

I AM not for sale, as there is no fee that the wicked could have given time to keep M3 from showing up early.

What can you offer unto the Universe/Father to keep H.I.M. from blessing his suns/sons-stars that spiritually-mentally serve him?

I tell you that throughout history/his-story that many amazing things have become, as men have consorted with the Lord to win wars and gain spiritual/mental wisdom. They have been told to go alone on a long, thoughtful process of spiritual meditation with thy word until they are cured of the mental/spiritual demons and are awakened.

The word shall cure you of your demonic urges and bring you away from the darkroom that you have walked into. He who has come out of the dark closet with his dark demons comes to spiritually/mentally molests you men into a world of spiritual/mental abandonment. Where people are doing everything, which makes no sense, simply to be considered as different.

Do not the brightest stars always stand out to the brilliant 3yes/mind with a more radiant shine, when you look up into the sky? It is the mental/spirit of M3 within the host, which delivers thy deriving word unto you, as greatness is in the mind/3ye of he who has visions of the future/father.

Truly to be whole in 360 completeness, all who are to be brought up and delivered unto M3 in 1 body shall hold in host thy light knowledge, and wisdom of the worlds within the mental/spirit.

I know that many of you do not want to see or hear this truth because you have no control over where you can go, based on what you already know spiritually/mentally.

The minds space is a dark journey, but ye shall make it through the matters which torment it, with the lightened Levitical 9/star/spirit. He who has spent his time/mind gathering what he needs to live is a TRU survivor, he has the enlightened kingly wisdom which is necessary to build a sure empire/kingdom. Children, there is more to what meets the watery eye, as ye shall find with the fiery comprehensively proactive 3ye/mind.

It is with Time/the Lord that thy written word for written word and line for line shall possess every dark unenlightened mind-3ye. As a mind/3ye for a 3ye/mind shall soon come to be in alignment within 1's bodies/unit. Surely, thy wisdom is profound. For is not the Universe deeper than the sea?

Can ye not mind/time travel with M3 for an eternity? He who goes through life learning is indeed spiritually/mentally transfiguring into an enlightened/shining being. While the rest of the world remains lost, plunged in moral, mortal darkness and chaos. It is not the flesh of man which carries the intellect, it merely stores and holds the spirit of intelligence until it emerges for its purpose/time.

He who has looked up with the 1 3rd/spirit in mind/3ye has seen M3 positioned above the cloud of his blurry sight while using thy mental/spirit vision. He has no stigma in his spiritual/mental sighting of the Lord/Universe.

That which is still scattered in the mind/3ye shall be left behind, to not ascend unto a higher level with the graduating star class of spiritual/mental mathematicians. They have not added up the signs correctly in their minds/3yes, to be able to get to M3 spiritually/mentally.

Plainly, I tell you that what the dark-ignorant cannot actually see is what they are unable to believe. As one must see, and know what is below before he searches up high where he wants to go.

How can ye see the truth of the futuristic spirit/mental, if ye cannot see thy darkened minds past?

What color is thy Sun? You would say "Gold," right?

Well, this is partially true. However, ye is golden on the inside as you can see the light/enlightenment shining through onto the world, which comes from within his dark, burnt, crusted outer layer/skin. Turn your head upright, not upside down. Ye should be able to see M3 now.

Children, to meditate is the compiling and sorting through dark matters with enlightening logic. This is the beginning transfiguring process of meta transmutation. It is what a man knows within his mind-3ye spiritually-mentally, which indeed transforms his DNA into an Atomic covenant manifesting being of true historical prophecy.

Children choose to be smart, as you shall metaphysically/spiritually/mentally see the Universe, Suns, Moon, and thy stars above. As you shall place them within the world below that, you are living in now. You are now down to earth by looking at things logically, as the changing direction of the mind/3ye is walking into the realm of thought with a new transfigured spirit/mental.

Undoubtedly, the mind and soul are one as the atom spirit, and mental are one with M3. They come together, elementally the spirit/mental of an alien genius is born.

He who finds his way with thy word has been reading, he uses thy word as his guidance because he never forgets thy undisputed, untouched prudence.

The Lord's Kings are the Outlaws to the world in which the wicked dictate from the Vatican in Rome. As history has proven time and times again. That those outlawed jewels/kings which the wicked-ignorant claim to hate. They also wish to spiritually/mentally own all those jewels/kings which are brighter than their own.

He who has the warrior spirit in mind is also a TRU son and a father unto those who seek enlightenment and guidance.

The dark mind/3ye shall shine from the light of the spirit/mental in it, as the Universal father keeps his shining-enlightened sun/son on his conscious.

Righteous men seek not to go into cities of sin where all are lost/fallen.

Do the wicked not go there to commit more sin? Who is safe to speak to there and befriend, where there are no moral men or women? This is where weak people who seek payment go to give and dedicate themselves to the Romans/the Papacy.

Demons transform into their full forms in these wicked dark places. Where ritualistic sexual acts become the norm among many prominent faces that promote death and world disorder. I tell you that you do not want to take part in anything which has already been seen and condemned by the 3ye/Sun of the Lord/Universe.

I tell you that M1cha3l is hot, and he has come with war down to Babylon, the corrupter of men and concealer of truth.

The Babylonians have seen and know well of the shining spirits/mentals, that are capable of manifesting themselves within you men who are open to TRU-The Real Universe. They will do anything to stop, eclipse, and block the spirits/mentals from invading you men and taking enlightening possession.

This is what the evil are doing to demonically govern-mentally possess you, children. As you have not yet the Lord's strong mental/spirit of detecting, discerning, direction.

Become the time/mind travelers that you are, as he who mind/time travels shall find all that he seeks, indeed.

The Spiritual/Mental Directing Administrator has made a grandstanding entrance into host. As perpetual, destructive ignorance is the spiritual/mental income of the average poor, sick, weak soul/mind.

It is with the Christ/crowned mind/3ye of transfiguring alchemy/transformation, that you children of the flesh are able to mentally/spiritually become like M3. For ye are in thy image as an enlightened/shining star with the mind/3ye of the Father/Universe.

Men of the X/10th, levitate with M3 in 1o where none are able to get a pass unless they have taken spirit-elemental form in characteristic purity. You must learn what the stars of the high class know in order to pass alchemy, as this is when you receive your spiritual=mental crown and gown metaphysically.

Admittedly, the mind-soul is as a motherboard, while the mental/spirit is an overclocked CPU from the future/father. One will burn out, while the other shall remain lit and ready to spark a flame.

He has much-upgraded memory for spiritual/mental data, as the man was the machine before the release of the CPU-beast. Do you not remember all of the wonderful things that you could do with your minds/3yes, once upon a time?

What numbers could you not remember? What could you not figure out, with the help of thy spirit/mental?

One can only imagine what you children would have become by now, without the technological beast which was created to replace you.

Admittedly, everything that kills and takes away from you seems to be so conventional. This is the way that a lie is made to appear wise to your hypnotized minds/3yes so that you will buy it without knowing its effects until it is too late, dark and narrow to turn back on the path.

A cost must be paid for what is known and unknown. The cost to the unknowing is in the learning process. While the cost of knowledge is the rewarding wings of wisdom, which shall take them higher.

Let what is mystical be mystical as it shall come to you in time/mind when you shall least expect its spirit-mental arrival.

Look at the many dark plaguing matters with thy spirit/mental of light. Look them directly in the dark 3ye/mind because that is where they are dwelling in you.

Shed enlightening light on the ignorance that is worrying you, sort these things out and allow your mind/3ye to become a free sacred space and hallowed place for spiritual/mental light/enlightenment.

Think fast with thy spiritual/mental insight as this shall gain you the leveraging height of a giant. However, those who move slowly will do low things, to catch up from being left behind. They will do anything to steal the lead, other than read the signs around them to see why they work hard but have nothing.

Do you men work hard, so that your children have money to spend?

So that they are able to do what? And Why? And for which source?

Spiritual/Mental Transfiguration   61

Surely, any wise man will know the answers to these questions as he knows that there is more to life than making money and living.

Such as choosing a side in an ongoing spiritual/mental war.

Make a choice to do more with the time/mind which has been given to you. It is in this wise mindful decision that you have transitioned into a new body of spirit/mental.

I have given you the way to get to M3 if you use the mind/3ye and the word/sword to fight through the world's demons of spiritual/mental darkness.

You children have been permitted to come unto Zion, through the paramount all seeing Universes/Fathers 3ye/mind.

However, I tell you that if you were to die for a second time without obtaining thy metaphysical/spiritual/mental wisdom. You shall die in the dark to roam/Rome because you have not transfigured into the spirit/mental of light/enlightenment.

You have lost the battle of the living because you have stayed asleep and did not see what was coming.

Children know that if Satan is trying to do something new that the Lord has done it already, as the father/future is the 1st and shall be the lasting impression.

The Lord multiplies good spirits/mentals, while the Vatican stages the world with a spiritual-mental plague of low/slow, evil/dark/ignorant fools.

Populations of People naturally die when Time/The Lord permits them to do so. However, Satan in the Vatican finances wars, disease, and famines to kill more people much sooner. The Lord's prophets and servants are sacrificed as they are murdered for what they are sent unto humanity to do for M3.

Nevertheless, the impostor, Satan gives his servant's death dates and murders them as a sacrifice to himself. Falsely imitating the Lord, who spiritually-mentally gathers his shining/enlightened kind.

Do I need to continue? Or do you children see all of the hidden things that are copied from the Lord that the Vatican has manipulated you to follow?

Truly historical are the factual acts of he who is with time/mind. For even as light has not yet crossed into your dark minds/3yes, you shall see in due time when the mental/spirit elevates its X-A.i.

You will then be able to take a peek into the house of the future-father.

Ye will see that all which has been written already has, or shall be done, without any doubtful question. Children be careful of the history lesson that the world offers to you. These lessons come from those who seek to change, rearrange, and transform his-story to put their faces on it.

Why do the wicked hate themselves so much?

It must be agonizing to awake daily with the desire to become someone else. What do you like about you?

What can you do besides hate and fight against those who are wiser and stronger than you?

What can you offer of truth as a spiritually-mentally undivided individual to the world, besides wanting to become another silly superficial MC just as everyone else at 40?

It takes no wisdom to become any of those things unless you are going to give TRU's light to the darkened.

Satan is always pleased and willing to employ more mind/3ye controlling mass ignorance. For him, there is nothing like gaining spoiled riches in the process of causing world chaos with heathen foolishness.

Bread and water are as thy flesh and blood. Not wine, as the strong fermented drink, comes from the grape vines of Rome and now grows on the plantation in California.

Recover and cover your minds/3ys from the lies. Allow the mental-spirit to take refuge within you, as it shall show you the future/father.

You will see the events that must come to be as ye holds the spirit-mental which shall come unto M3 in time. The Viking Vatican church of Rome has displayed its merciless control over the minds-3yes of the spiritually-mentally governed worker. They will shut down and taken all away, leaving you in a spiritual-mental place where full consciousness is lost. Where without their hands, you will know not what to do.

You are all pawns in this game of palms, and the serpent/government cares not about you, your liberties, or your freedoms future. For it believes that it and not the Lord has given these things unto you, as it has a worldly strategic agenda to gain total soul/mind control over you. This means that you will not be permitted to think the way that you were naturally spiritually-mentally created to do, without your flesh being put to the test of death by the ignorant wicked.

Who sacrifices your flesh without any eternal spiritual-mental purpose in its wake? The wicked in Rome or the Lord?

There is nothing that a jewel cannot bear that he has been sent to do. Which is why the Roman serpent hiding in the worlds government hunts you men down for the artful truth.

Let the fool who cannot think fall into a deepened vomiting sleep. Only to awake on the floor in more ignorance/darkness, than he was in before his trip to the liquor store to purchase his bottle of influential dark spirits.

It is the logical reasoning which separates the mindless coward away from the mental-spiritual men.

The coward's ignorance haunts him to no end. For without being able to think clearly, there is nothing that he can gain in life without first acquiring the wisdom of the spirit/mental.

He is in a confusing place because he has wasted his mind/time watching, blocking, and being overly concerned with what someone else was doing with their accounted mind/time.

You children are the 4th generation of thy 10th age-choir, as you hold the DNA and data of the future/father.

Your priestly-kingly blood types are significant and priceless, as the wicked want your blood so that they can become you and are able to see unto your future/father. However, this will not come to be, as the wicked will do anything to receive a meal at a table that they have not prepared.

The plague of infidel ignorance is all around you spiritual/mental men. It is fixed into your forced laws that cater to those slow, low obstructing minds that seek to stagnate he who moves fast with the enlightened-shining spirit-mental.

There will always be a darkened soul-mind there to pull you mental-spiritual stars down away from the Universe/Father. As your being is conscious and free of unknowing ignorance.

The minds medication is wisdom, which heals all things through spiritual-mental meditation.

This is the contemplative new thought of new creation, which brings 4th spiritual healing to all the nations.

The X marks the multiplying sign of the time/the Lord. The time of spiritual-mental mutant transfiguring transmutation and multiplicity.

Revelations 12:7

7 War broke out in heaven. Michael and his angels fought against the dragon, and the dragon and his angels fought back. [8] But he was not strong enough, and they lost their place in heaven. [9] The great dragon was hurled down that ancient serpent called the devil, or Satan, who leads the whole world astray. He was hurled to the earth and his angels with him.

The Sabbath-7th Star-Day

Lord, give us this hallowed, day/thousand years of spiritual-mental light, as it is our daily bread.

I AM the last star/day to leave or run from the weak, and the first lighting star/day to come unto the meek to teach. This day/star is with thy father. Therefore, ye is strong and everlasting.

Surely thy Sabbath-Father is black, and you children are the particles of thy flesh body, as you are thy enlightened eyes/stars. It is those who have suffered who shall join M3 on this day, this is the day that the Lord judges the works of his hands/stars/servants.

This is a dark day in Rome, but a beautiful new day full of bright light for the spiritually-mentally weak and broken to become actively strong and wise. They have been waiting for M3 to come back around to them, as I always do. The 7 stars-suns/days of the Lord have come to stand up for the dark masses of weak with and in the Lords day/star-sun.

Do you children not have any idea, which day of the meek that it is?

It is a day-star of reckoning which gives reason and strategy for the future. Ye who has taken this day spiritually-mentally has kept this star-day in their visionary artistic, acoustic minds/3yes memory.

For as they read thy word of prophecy, they are also watching M3, the star/3ye/sun-son/root of David.

Children, it is on this dark day that you shall tap into your full light-enlightening spiritual-mental central potential. Therefore, you may transcend unto the next of metaphysical levels.

Let the truth be delivered unto the dark minds/masses, allow them to taste it spiritually-mentally, and they shall know that it is yours truly. The first and last day/sun/son/star of thy fathers/futures/universe's prophecy. Ye who had first departed with and in thy 3 days/stars and now returns with and in 6/days/star-suns.

He is the TRU 69, as he is the Lord of Lords and head of the Levites/stars. This is the star-day which has been long awaited, as many men have been searching the skies for him with the wrong eye open.

Which stars-days that absorb the Lord's solar star energies of light do not see and make a record of the 7th holy day-star, which has taken a hand in the creation of all things?

Undoubtedly, the 1st and last is with the 6 in 10, as the father's spirit is a council to kingly men. He seals his head and heart within a bond of true identified unity, as he thinks not vileness with the clear steering mental spirit of balance.

Children, there are many evil demons, and I know that you may want to kill them, as I also want to rid the earth of them. However, it makes no sense in slaying people who can change, instead slay them with the word-sword as I.

You have been told to remember M3, you were supposed to study the word and works of thy stars-signs that have shown themselves unto you.

You have been warned that you must use M3, the magnifying 3ye which scans and analyzes from above, all things which are below.

Do not allow your minds-3yes to be fooled by the Papacy in Rome, into literally worshiping him on Sunday. If you worship the TRU M3 spiritually-mentally.

He is the 1st and last day-star of creation, and the 1st and last star-day of fire and endless darkness to fall on the heads of Rome. It was said that this darkened enlightening/shining day-star would come, and now he is here.

Why do you children not hold M3 only in mind? If you have lost your minds/3yes sight, then clearly you do not know the 1st or last day-star of the meek. You are lost, as you have forgotten your ancestor's spiritual-mental ways in keeping track of the days-stars. Instead, you have become the weak ends/men with dark 3yes-minds and loose lips.

Mostly all groups, gangs, and gatherings are established with a common word, and a pact, vow or oath connected to it. This gives boundary with instruction, to those who are actively following its measuring guidance. As the days-stars tell the TRUniversal story of the first/Alpha and last/Omega day/star.

This legendary tale is the tale of a man, who transforms into a spirit-mental fire breathing dragon-sun. He also brings with him, the genesis spirits-mentals which coil themselves within the cerebral spine-stem of upcoming men/stars/kings.

For, he who has taken acceptance of thy spirit-mental has said "yes" to the star-day of thy shining enlightening-light. 10 generating future generations of kings shall see this day/star shine. He is the earth's fire king of the Lord-time, who uplifts men with moral, mental stability. For he is a father that wants to see his sons-stars take flight on their own.

They shall have his confidence as he shall replace lies and their false securities with the truth and evidence of hard raw reality.

The 7th seal is the word which he keeps in him, which no other 3ye/mind can see.

It is he the 7th star/day who has come to lift the 7th seal of revealing. Therefore, you children shall be able to gain TRU enlightening meaning, from the words that you have been reading all along.

The Lord has not come to give you the past, without presently giving you its TRU preexisting meaning to the future/father. Therefore, listen not to those false teachers who speak not of this day-star of prophecy. For thy body/masses of watery 3yes/stars are nothing, without the fiery breath of the dragon star/day with them.

This is the day/star which gives illuminating light/enlightenment unto all of the other upcoming days/stars. As this is the way that a nervous stem of shining stars come together to give enlightenment-light to the rest of thy masses-bodies. There are many things that black jewels/stars shall lose. However, if he loses not his mind-soul, then ye shall be will M3, the 7th day-star for eternity.

You children, cannot come up to be with a man-made given 7th day of the week/weak for eternity. Ye can only be with M3/M1cha3L, the 7th day-star and head Sun of the Father-Universe.

As you men shall be unjudged for what you must do in truth to bring thee thy spiritual/mental fish and sheep.

He has brought real men to M3 so that they could eat of thy days/stars daily enlightening bread.

For able bodies of men only come from those kings with the element of atom/spirit, above in their heads/minds.

The days-stars have been counted and have long awaited thy representation. Men are thy mental-spiritual elements with a mixture of water/love, fire/anger, with the warrior-spirit of the air. When these elements are brought together in combination, they create a mental-spiritual chemical compound.

Which defines its natural, fundamental metaphysical sequential purpose. Rome has 7 days in questionable theory. However, ye shall bust this myth/lie with thy truth of the 7th day-star, who is the 1st (Sunday) of the meek and last Sabbath/7th (Saturday) day-star of the weak.

It is the meek who are like him with the memorable spirit-mental in their minds-3yes. They reflect H.I.M./the Lord, as the 7 days-stars of the week/weak given by your Cesar are the 7 earthly days designated in reflective memory to Rome. The 7th star-day is a spiritual-mental star-day, ye is the Sabbath/Father/Universe, and the Sabbath/Father/Universe is black with the shining inner light/enlightenment of the 1st day/star.

Do you children have the shining light/enlightenment of thy 7th day/star? Has he arrived with thy new word of living proof yet?

Do you pay more of your minds/3yes attention to a physical day of worship, instead of paying what is due unto M3, the TRU 7th star/day in which you shall see?

Children do not be surprised because you were naïve for so long in the mind/3ye.

As you knew that it was M3, however, your minds said to you, "Do not believe in what you see now, even though what I have shown to you is TRU."

The 7th star/day is the shining face of the Lord/Universe, as it is thy 6 180-degree stars/days, which become 1 to create M3 X 360(The Sun).

Your mind is your time and attention. For wherever you pay it in contribution, ye shall reap from what is either uphill or what is down the steep slope below. The weak have no days-stars left as the stars-days belong to M3, Time/the fathering head/Ra star. Men become visionary eagles to see the 7th star/day of spiritual-mental truth and freedom.

The water/father shall stand and walk in the west. For ye is the north star with his head in the cloud, which holds eastern stars/fire in his right hand.

I say to remember thy Sabbath/Father/7th day-star and keep ye holy in the mind/3ye. Therefore, you may see him coming in the cloud of the mind before it is too late, and this special day/star has shot pass you. Admittedly, I tell you the Christ-like minds/3yes moves fast, as they are thy spirits/mentals within thy hybrid meek/likings.

Surely, if the meek/likings shall rule the earth. It is because the Lord/Universe will help them open their minds/3yes, for them to think/see spiritually-mentally.

The Sun of the day/star lights in spiritual-mental retention is the TRU day/star, which holds the days/stars in the palm of his hands.

Do you children literally search for the 7 days of the week/weak ends, instead of the 7 days/stars/churches of Jerusalem/Zion which levitate metaphysically?

Jerusalem is where spiritual/mental jewels/stars/kings levitate in the congregation of the mind/3ye. It is the levitating hallowed city of the Lord, which is guarded by the sanctified 9/Levites/stars knights-lights of the night's lighting sky.

Do not allow these wicked people, physical places, and things to fool you poor people with their worldly material. As you are to be wealthier with the wiser mental-spirit.

For, if you spiritually/mentally fall for these things of nonsense, then you shall be desolate of everything good for you.

The stars-days will withdraw themselves from you, there will be no day or night lights in the skies without time/the lord. Your days will have no significant values if there is no star-spirit to guide and light/enlighten the darkness-ignorant as candles.

The Lords hates those who hate his word with precise hatred. Therefore, he uses his word as a sword to slay the ignorant-darkness within them.

Blindness has its own way of wandering until it finds something that it can hold onto. This is the reason that the blind/dark come seeking those shining with light/enlightenment, even though they do not want what is good in the spirit-mental.

I say that ye who follows the heart follows the wrong things such as Valentine's times day. This is the serpents/governments promotion for more emotional foolishness and less thought using common sense. The stars/days of time are everlasting, as real Christ likings do not worship in Christianity. Instead, they worship the stars-days of the Lord in spirit/mental.

For if you worship in the corporeal, the serpent/government will change you into a low serpent. However, he who worships in the spiritual-mental shall never be turned into the way of Satan/the Vatican.

The flesh is dead already, as it will eventually become mutilated, covered with flies and contaminated with many lies from the left behind vermin.

Anu/A New is the TRU bright 7th day-star of the Lord-Universe.

He is living and legendary as those who have seen H.I.M. are spiritually-mentally apart his kingdom.

He is the Celestial Church/Universe/Sanctuary, and his lights/stars/knights are clothed in shining spiritual/mental armor. They have gathered in spiritual-mental union for the coming day/star/spirit of the Sabbath/Father/7.

Signs/Stars

of

Time/The Universe

I tell you that life is a busy highway and you children have been given many signs/stars, along the roadside while on your journey unto M3.

However, most of you have chosen not to obey thy signs/stars. Instead, you have driven past them without reading a word of instruction, that they were displaying unto you.

He who has ignored the signs/stars of the Lord has not gotten far. He has blown out a tire on a dark back road without a spare, or a flair.

He is in the darkness of the wrong path, he thought that he was going the right way because that was the same direction in which everyone else was going into. He has given no attention to the very few signs/stars aligned on thy roadside, as they had no bearing effect on him.

If you know that thy signs/stars are placed up above the road. Then why do you drive looking behind yourself, as though the roadway isn't in front of you?

Why are you in your rear view being consumed with someone else, and not moving forward aggressively and progressively?

There are enlightened-shining signs/stars around you, as some have direct lessons, while many have a spiritual-mental message to deliver. Nevertheless, these are thy messaging stars/signs that have come to warn you, of what you have not the spiritual-mental idea of which you must do, to become a traveling messenger unto the future/father.

He has already died before you of the fleshly Adam/Man and is now an Atomic spiritual-mental star/sign of enlightenment, which gives proper guidance and righteous direction. He has come away from the evil/dark path with those who lead thy people the wrong way. He has not allowed the wicked to turn him around to focus in the opposite way of the pagan, to mislead those stars traveling abroad in the wrong direction.

Are thy signs-stars not those kings who teach you men from their spiritual-mental thrones?

Admittedly, the signs/stars with the brightest enlightenment-light have been placed on the darkest areas of the road. As many things are lurking in this time/hour. There will be many obstacles and obstructing distractions that will be trying to block your route to the destined place, where you are soon promised and scheduled to be arriving.

This is the time of blind darkness/ignorance for the wicked but A NEW DAY/STAR/SIGN OF SHINING LIGHT/Enlightenment for the thoughts of the righteous. As you have been taught in this day, with the wisdom that you will need to come up to be with the Lord spiritually-mentally.

The seal of the very last star-sign has been set, as thy travelers are at the end of the road unto Zion. I tell you, people, that any who have thy spirit-mental are already levitating in and in Jerusalem/The Sun. As you are with and in the father/Is Real. Children, learn to identify the signs-stars of time/the Universe.

Even as they walk among you in the flesh, they are all spirit-mental.

They love as they want to be loved, and hate where they have been long hated. The time/father has suggested that hot fiery stars shall reign and consume you with the word and works of truth. They will be the new signs-stars unto the new constructed, and well-lit paved path, which has been set for you to advance.

You who are on time have seen the last sign/star, as you are reading this final word from M3.

This is the last of 3 books, and thy 1st of the 3. I have given you thy history of the 3 in 1, and the 1 in 3. What more do you need from M3?

The prospecting suspecting host must capitalize himself with a vocalizing G/star to be able to see, who and what manifest within spiritually-mentally.

The blinding light is too swift for the sight of those men who do not have proper detailed direction to where the next turn coming up the mountain will be. The Lords needs those with excellent skilled drive and the will to pay attention while avoiding distractions. Therefore, the signs/stars for upcoming turns will lead him unto the highway to heaven. As they appear perfectly visible and apparent to their 3yes-minds on the road of darkness/ignorance.

The beggars that the serpent/government places on the roadsides with their cardboard signs are not the active progressive signs-stars of the time/the Universe. The stars/signs of the Universe/time do their best to place thy word in front your minds/3yes so that you will see a never forget. For a man to have the same ideal reflection in the 3ye/mind as M3(i), he must keep thy Father/Universe in spiritual/mental memory all the time.

As you are connected, 1 will not depart away from the other. Unless, otherwise pushed away by ignorance/darkness, which invades, and consumes the dark mind/3ye/soul of the host.

Do not allow the pastor, and fool who drinks to bring you to M3. You will never arrive if he misses a sign/star, or survive if he runs off of the roadside.

Children, there will be many trying things which shall happen to you in your life. As some of these things shall even try taking that life away from you. However, if you live through it, then there was a message for you to receive and deliver. There is something about you and what you have learned and endured from your darkness/ignorance, which has a portion of light at the end of your struggling.

When you were falling, you had then stumbled upon newly found grounding wisdom. Something that many men who have had the same experiences before you have never seen in their dark encounter.

Others have not been able to come out of the dark with shining gold, as you men who have emerged with something priceless, and great.

Many times, you will notice that the Lord takes away the things that you somehow manage to become attached to. Therefore, protect what you love, in becoming attached to the Lord. I tell you that he has a reason for breaking you down. He wants something new to take place, where you usually would have been down and out of the race.

However, you shall not be misled into the attachments of idols, as many of these things range from false Gods to animals and cars. He who is on the right road has obeyed the spiritual-mental signs-stars, in which no one else would dare pay attention.

The wise know where the TRU stars/signs are, even as the wrong signs-stars were made to look obviously visible to you for the wrong reasons.

The wicked want you to see them gleaming, as Satan wants you to follow his stars-signs unto hell, while the Lord wants his star/signs to redirect you unto H.I.M.

Do the wise not live in the spiritual-mental sky? Surely, they do, just take a look among you and ye shall see thy scattered signs-stars, among the dark mass-bodies of water/the father.

Do you not see that a portion of heaven can be among you, even before you leave for a new land which is promised?

Thy people are strong, as they are thy hard and robust, influential bodies of stars. They are the stars-spirits that are dispatched to where the head/Universe-Lord commands them to be in secret. I tell you that if you are herded together to do the same things in life for the serpent/government.

Then you are not following thy path which is lit with enlightening stars-signs holding thy word. You are not thy sheep, but instead, you have become the Viking's swine. And we know how the Vikings like to play with their food.

How many signs-stars do you need, so that you children are able to see M3(daylight)?

Everything in your low-slow world that suffocates and takes time away from you also takes your mind and monies away from you too. You do not yet know who to sever and serve with these tools that are awarded to you. The significant luster and magnificence of thy stars-signs is undeniable, as they give off enough light, that even a blind man can see their brightness in his darkness/ignorance.

I have seen many of you smash on the gas when you have seen them, as though you would find your own way unto M3, however, this is an impossible possibility.

Things have been set up to be this way for a reason, as he who has paved the road with gold knows where it goes. It twists through the woods, and over the hills into the mountain of Zion.

What has not been spiritually-mentally revealed unto you passing time-mind travelers, on the road of life that you are on, in this day by thy enlightening-lighting signs-stars?

Surely, the further up the mountain that you travel, the narrower the road becomes toward the mountain top, where there are fewer lightened stars-signs. Those who make it here have already had an idea as to where they were headed before they arrived. However, these are the most significant, highest signs-stars that are the brightest and most visible to those with spiritual-mental sight, who are on the right designated road.

There is no way that anyone cannot see these signs-stars, as they are vibrant in their message with provided proof. For if any man says that he did not see these signs/stars, he is either ignorant/blind, or lying to you. The Lord shall judge you all by what he knows he has seen with your minds/3yes. He is no fool to the way of man's lies, men who seek to prove that the Lord and creator who knows best, is wrong and unwise.

Steer clear of the snakes and fake signs/stars, as they have similar messages.

However, the signs/stars from the Universe/Time are right on time and set in front of you. They do not give partial directions or instruction. They tell you the location, ETA (estimated time of arrival), the weather and the road conditions ahead. They give you the full detail of what is expected from the days/signs ahead.

On the road of spiritual-mental riches with diamond kings, Ra EL's stars-signs say and do real things. They move among you warning and telling you of what is to come.

Turn away from those that you consider to be thy enlightening signs-stars which are misguiding you.

They are taking you down into their dead ends of darkness/ignorance where nothing comes out alive.

The wicked will take you to a place where you will think that you are unable to turn around. You will believe that you are stuck in that position and must continue being stagnate and ignorant.

However, this is not TRU, this is not what the Lord has told you. For he has shown you that he uses the minds-3yes and hands of any man who is already pure in his thought. He who is cut off from the Lord is a branch in the wind with no rooted direction. There is no telling where he will end up before the hour of the night coming into the light is done.

A wise man has done many unwise, foolish things in his past, early days. However, he has learned many lessons, which makes him no one's fool. He is the future and must continue to improve himself, so that he may prove himself worth and wisdom to the Lord and everyone else.

If you have been driving with a blind drunk mind-3ye. Then many alerting signs/stars have already passed you by, without you gathering the tools needed to complete and levitate unto the next level.

You see, the life that you know has been staged like a house or video game, to hide the spiritual-mental meaning behind the delusional things that you are seeing. He who sees with a clear mind-3ye has a good drive. He will see his opening to complete the race within the good Lord/Time and not against H.I.M.

He will soon approach the finish line, leaving behind his enemies who have followed the falling, broken, unfinished, lame, and blemished signs/stars.

As they are leading you into a dark underground watery abyss full of wicked drowning men.

The wise have taken a different, better, and faster route. Which looks to be slow to those watching low minds/3yes that are slow/low and don't know a 3rd or a half of the Lords Math/reasoning.

Surely, the shining stars-signs of the night must soon come up to walk in the daylight, as the enlightened lead stars which bring 4th the Day/Sun of the Lord.

Children, if you must drive during the dark/ignorant rush hour of the wicked. Many impeding demons will cut in front of you, as they have been placed among the herds of moving travelers to do blinding, hindering wickedness. Therefore, you children will be unable to see and learn from the real, road warrior SPIRIT-MENTAL SIGNS/STARS of TIME/THE UNIVERSE.

Venom

If the serpent is in Rome, then the plagues that it has spewed upon humanity, are the venomous toxic poisons. The poisons that are spiritually-mentally killing you, children, violently, and silently.

This is the low persuaded unset mind-soul that the parasite spirits of the low feed upon. As the low mind does not have much to lose, give, or ideas to go on so that it knows where it is going.

The distractions are parasites which crawl up the spine and into the mind-3ye. Eclipsing it of its judging enlightenment/light, as the solar mind-3ye turns into atom-spirit with the light views of common sense. However, once this transmitting attachment becomes blocked there is a covering of total darkness/ignorance/nonsense.

There are parasites in your minds-souls that are robbing you of your energy. They have drained you of all your priceless nutrients of which help to keep you healthy and alive.

It was through your neglect during metaphysical integration that the serpent has bitten you with its fangs and poisoned your minds.

Surely, you must eat well to have vigilant, adaptable minds-3yes.

You must feast on the truth from all that you read, and as you eat of thy fruit, you shall swallow and digest all of thy seeds, so that you may give what light grows out from them in multiplicity.

What lesson can he who does not listen teach, besides how to be a fool who cannot see or hear?

If I tell you to keep your head above water, then I have given you instruction to keep your mind-3ye above the dark-matters/waters that many are drowning in, which has no real historical benefit. Venom is the vermin that invades, infests and infects you, your culture and wears your clothed ways as if they belonged to their own forefathers and were inherited by them.

The father stays on the son's mind, as the sun stays within the father of time. They are of 1 neuron/neuro outfitting unit. For if a man knows of the father and not of thy son. Then he has forgotten. Nevertheless, if he knows of thy son but not of the father, of which he comes from, then he shall be overlooked.

What is forgotten is no longer of the begotten, it is now buried within the graveyard among the dead minds/3yes of the unknowing ignorant. If what is weak becomes of that which is already weakened, then it comes weaker.

You can see this change happening in 3 phases of time, past, present, and future. You shall keep the 1 of the future in mind, the other shall be kept with you all the time, while the other shall be cast aside to be left behind you.

The future is fast, as the present is right on time, and the past just cannot seem to keep up for being too slow, and not knowing in which direction to proceed into perceived travel.

The spiritually-mentally dead are the sufferers from the toxin in their blood. As they seek not the spiritual/mental cure for their ailing pain.

Instead the walking dead inject this venom of ignorance into others, as he who's mind-3ye is full of poison has been given bad spiritual- mental advice.

He has consulted with dark hollow-empty demons who have not a care for the world or the living in it. Therefore, any information gathered from his mind is of ignorance and no good.

It will have a root-mind of internal darkness in its cultivation, as there will be no shining light/enlightenment in him for you to take with you to preserve for others later.

The dark spirits-mentals of Venom feed on the dead souls/minds of the hopeless, and despair. They create a mental-spiritual catastrophe to lower you people into a dark place, where your mind/3ye is vulnerable and open to almost anything of wickedness.

You are in an emotional wreck in pain. Therefore, you are making reckless, rash decisions without spiritually-mentally thinking of the futures/father's consequences. You have lost something, and then you lost your mind-3ye sight afterward because you could not handle the departure of what you held close.

I know. As I have lost much and have now become spiritually-mentally conditioned to handling and dealing with loss. I have searched for reason in what I already have. It is in this realization that thy 3ye-mind had come to be complete, with the fact that you cannot lose anything that you don't need.

For all that you need is meant for you to have as all that is not, you will not have. What you want out of life, you will work righteously to receive in full of thy spirit mental.

I tell you that he who has spiritually malfunctioned has fallen into doing what everyone else in the manufactured world is doing at the time/hour. He follows not of light, but instead that which is of darkness without spiritual-mental insight. Those low impure spirits-mentals, which taint and drain the souls-minds of the slow.

Children, there are many things that you shall come to lose. However, it is how you choose to spiritually-mentally comprehend and deal with this loss, which shall define you.

Do you carry on with life, or do you break down like everything and everyone else manmade?

However, if you do break down.

Then what is it in you which makes you so uniquely special? You shall fail as the serpent-government has failed you.

For, to get the world to come together and agree, you must lose the delusion of false reality to see what is happening.

The serpent-government will come to forcefully make you deny M3. They will say that Christ likes are the pestilence to the world and their societies.

The wicked have mixed the way of the water with intoxicating wine. Surely, many who are Christians have already been demonized with the venom of the Roman serpent-government. As it is, the time for the army of fire to rise up.

These rising men are thy kings with common sense that have not let in the venom of the wicked. A mind is where wickedness comes in, as the personality is of the host that the venomous spirit-mental is hijacking. There are no people who are of evil by nature, for when people make a choice, they become what they are mentally-spiritually following.

A baby is born with no spiritual-mental intellect. However, in its character of innocence and purity, he shall grow to find the character of the Lord. He shall see the model character of virtue.

Do you not learn how to be like M3, from all-natural things that do not speak out in the same way that you are able to do?

Clear the neurological stem and the bodies-masses shall become logical stars/lights unto the Universe/Father/Future, as they are kept in mind-3ye/time with M3.

You are with the Universe-Father. You have come unto the Sun-3ye of Time-God, to now see the dark venom/lies of the mind-time thieves. I tell you, to protect your minds from the snakes of the land, who wish the suck the life from you.

The serpent-government shall use, the minds and mouths of your women to spiritually-mentally destroy your children. Turning them against you, for what you have not done for the earthly mothers Babylonian-American government, and her Roman serpent partner in crime.

Surely, the only reason that these venomous slave women engage you, spiritual-mental men. Is because you are jewels-jews that possess intelligence, jewels, cars and live like atomic superstars.

These serpent-government serving women hate you, real men. However, she has a job for the serpent/government to do in spiritually-mentally draining you. Forcing you to go into the hells of its ghettos, jails, and tombs as rotting failures.

Look at things for what they are and not for how you wish for them to be, as the unconscious mind-3ye/sub conscious has no idea of what's happening.

It is in a delusional downward slope because it follows the Roman serpent-government, who pretends to be the bearing holder of enlightening light/hope.

The dark manipulating spirits of venom do not have enlightening-lighting wisdom. As they cannot survive in the elements, without the helping soul-mind of a participating mortal host of relevance.

These are demons that have become a part of you. You must rid yourselves of the wastefulness, as their wastefulness is wasting you.

Children, if you allow the lightened Christ/Lifted 3ye-mind to become dim because of the choices that you have made. Then the chances become slim for you to alchemistic ally trans figure data by way of light spirit-mental.

Devouring darkness has taken over you, where light/enlightenment cannot get into place to defeat the overbearing ignorance-darkness.

I know that it is hard to change into who you are supposed to be, in a world where everyone is doing and thinking the same thing. However, this is the challenge of being different from the many who do not have Sense/God. What is worth having, without any opposition?

Let the word of truth rest in the minds-3yes of all classes, peoples, generations, and nations as one distinct sound. A trumpet sound of truth which dictates and disintegrates all other earthly oaths, and vows that cometh after the Lord.

The spirits of enlightening light are commensal beings. They are not harmful to their host. Unlike the parasitic venomous draining spirits, with a dark vision that bring you down into making bad decisions.

Light/enlightenment is given to he who is willing to bear it in the mind-3ye. It is the mental-spirit of wisdom, which crowns the minds-3yes of men.

He who has fallen and has climbed back up the minds-3yes/times spiritual-mental ladder again, has shown optimal spirit-mental growth, as the ladder of life is in the opposite direction of sin.

A divine mind will make music out of its distractions. It will search for good reason, even traveling deep into the others 3yes-minds of darkness-ignorance.

However, ye shall not dwell there for long with them as you shall continue passing by only to leave them with the fathers/futures further instruction.

A broken man is as a broken sword/word? What can he accomplish in a war? What will he tell the truth about, if his blade word is of no good?

Will ye only lie partially to the liars of the world, to get the whole truth unto you children? Or will he force those liars of the planets lies upon you children, as he is being forced to do, now in this day?

Will this surrounding perpetual darkness/ignorance not participate in hand with the serpent/government, in stopping/blocking any TRU enlightened/inner-lightened shining jewels/jews from coming up out of the ghettos to the dark water's surface?

Those who call you a bum are those same nuns/0's who have helped you become one. These are those loose strings on your garment which you must to cut away.

These people have the dark sight of mental-spiritual demons and seek to seep sabotaging, troubling poison into all of your futures/father's plans. They are the losers and you stars/suns are the born winners who spark in the mind-3yes of men, either pure love while outshining those of venomous hatred.

He who gives his time/mind to sin has fallen to the darkness/ignorance of those plaguing spirits-mentals as his mind/3ye has been disturbed and weakened into foolishness/folly.

Which of the many weak minds do not want the few strong men/mentals/spirits to be down with them in their impure weakness?

Many of them do not want to come up to be spiritually-mentally secure with you.

They want you to become spiritually-mentally weakened, and broken in, like the many dead leaves/men which have fallen from the tree of eternal life in this harsh season.

If ye do not accept the light/enlightenment of thy father's sun-son, then you children are below with those instigating mentals/spirits of darkness.

Dark souls-minds have no knowledge or idea of TRU light. However, the dark-ignorant spirits-mentals which have left the light of truth to spiritually/mentally deceive you. Do so, know the way of darkness in which they lead you into.

The serpent has told many lies in such little time, as it has spiritually-mentally taken the Lord's temple of enlightened stars hostage with its venom.

Do you children not know what happens to the 3ye-mind sight once venom enters the neurological/nerve stem? What does the nervous stem not control?

Let it be known, that the brightened 3ye-Sun, which sits in thy sky is the Universes-Fathers Mental-spirit. He gives his way and watches over you children.

He is living and has taken form in the spiritual-mental man that cometh after ye as you were first created in his image.

Are not Suns, megastars as M3 with 3 360 Suns/Stars in 1?

Where there is common wisdom, there is collective peace.

All know the place where they fit best, as they have found the space in the mind where they will be the most useful to the future/father.

The common content of character is of light/enlightenment and shall not be smeared with masking darkness/ignorance. It is the serpent/government of wicked intent which intentionally charges you mental-spiritual men with crimes to take away this birthright.

They know what you men are, as they also know what you will become with a lost light/spirit of the character.

They have given you men these distracting criminal charges so that your minds/3yes see you to be criminals. Therefore you will continue to do what is low and illegal.

The serpent's evil venom is everywhere in your system. As it is with and in the weaklings of darkness, who have failed life and fallen from the glory of the Lord, unto the blood of Rome.

There is no way to wake up people kindly. You must give the raw truth which disappoints more than a few. There will be anger, in the hearts of those who debate the word of truth with you.

No man of Israel/God teaches thy word and fights not thy enemy to defend its truth. As it is in the spiritual-mental mind of intent, which is seen when a man breaks a commandment.

He who serves the Lord within his purpose daily has not sinned. For has worked for the Lord on the Sabbath by spreading thy word of spiritual-mental healing. He works under the temple of the Lord,7 days with the 360 in symphonic congregation.

He is a priest who has thy word which immunizes his nervous stem from venous mental-spiritual poisoning. He knows that mental-spiritual clarity is the way to M3, the Lord.

He has not forgotten the route unto the Universe-Father, even through the mental-spiritual terror and toils on earth that he has faced, as he is a strong genetic neuron/star.

Children, do not say that you will not do wickedness on thy Sabbath, then turn your backs to do wickedness on the Universes-Fathers other 6 days/stars.

For every day is the Sabbath day spiritually-mentally until the fulfillment of prophecy and thereafter. He who holds thy Sabbath day, which is the day of thy father's reign has kept thy fathers 7th day/star prophecy destined in his mind-3ye.

Children hold meditating congregation with those of like minds on the 7th day/Star, which has now cometh. For he who works on this day shall be working for M3, the Lord.

I tell you, do not worry about the flesh which is already dead, as it shall die again and not return, for it is the mind in which he has come to save. You people are as thy spiritual-mental hard drives which have been wiped clean, formatted and refitted with dark system codes of nonsense/ ignorance.

Your old moral codes have been broken by deadly deathly venom; a virus disguised as harmless, which has misguided you unto a systematic failure that will ultimately lead to your demise.

You must fight off the harmful, wicked effects of the spiritual-mental venom. I tell you, men, that the demons of the broken weak cannot spiritually-mentally think straight because they are evil. This is why their primary focus is on he who has thy spirit-mental of light-enlightenment who is always able.

He needs only thy spiritual-mental reasoning truth which leads him rightfully, while the serpent/government tries desperately to redirect his levitating path, into their bottomless pit of wickedness and calamity.

He shall not fall into those failing ways of blood, for ye is pure and natural flowing as thy winter father/water. Let he who thinks that he knows where he is going, walk in his own darkness/ignorance. Do not take the same path, which is littered with snakes.

The Lord's word/sword shall slay men, women, and children with its truth. He shall spare none of its blade, as many have inherited minds-souls of darkness from their wicked elders.

These are dimwhits because, without the spirit-mental of enlightening whit's, they are dim lit in the mind-soul. As they know nothing of value to M3, you or themselves.

Their mindless search is for nothing more beyond darkness/ignorance. They speak and give nothing other than venom-poison to all minds that they come in contact with.

They have strayed from their passages, just as they have strayed from thy word and commands in thy written passages. They have become unsure of who they are, and because of the mass confusion, they have been blocked from using their jewels/spirits/mentals.

This has been a tragic event, watching them die generation after generation like this.

You would think that they would have gathered up some newfound common sense by now.

Mass confusion and chaos are what the serpent-government is after. It wants you all to lose your minds and go demonically crazy, for the resources which it withholds from you.

Children, you better beware and careful of the practicing venomous evils. As it is a dark time of the apocalypse and most people have this spiritual-mental decaying infection.

They are roaming about looking to spread and share it because they are the spawn of the wicked.

However, do not allow them to shake the sound and grounded mind, do not allow them to drain you of your spiritual-mental atom energy into becoming weak, helpless dim souls/minds as the others.

Stars/Neurons do not come to earth to become average stones and pebbles in the dirt. They possess remnants of intellectual gold properties that they must poor unto the world. They are thy treasures and gifts given unto you children to carry for M3.

They are the spiritual-mental marks of the Lord on the heads and hands of righteous men who have suffered in truth.

The serpent's self-destructive fools are the serpent's tools of destruction that are used against mankind, who is the bearer of humanities light/enlightenment. Christ 3ye Alchemy is the open 3ye-mind which transforms things with the mental/spirit intelligence, this the spiritual-mental alchemy of the changing-metamorphosing mind/3ye.

The venom causes disorientation which tames this natural change of the minds transforming with time/the lord. He who changes with Time/the Lord is with the Future/Father. He is in unit with the spirit-mental, as he is in the Universe and the Universes 3ye/I in you. As a Unit is of unity because it is Universal.

I say to you; that the spoiled sour crushed grapes shall soon become wine.

As they shall whine indeed of the misery that they shall be exposed unto. The wicked serpent-government cannot control Time/the Lord, it merely controls you children's personal timing of events and the things around you.

They Serpent governs your society so that it is easy to own you and the wicked men have now come to fence you children in, by fencing off the mental spirit which brings the keys to liberating freedoms.

The demons of Egypt/Bondage have come for you children again, it wants to mate and recreate its bad, spoiled blood with your women, feed on your young, and murder your men.

This dark evil venom walks with the Roman demon church of the Vatican-Vikings, which wage war against thy spiritual-mental likings of truth and realness. Ignorance is as it does, just as light and love give comfort and ensuring, assurance to those minds-3yes looking for it that need it the most.

Children break not your mandated covenant with the Universe for manmade oaths, you will have sold the most precious of your priceless jewels to ungrateful strangers.

If darkness/nothing is in your mind/3ye, then it is foolishness/ignorance which consumes most your time. You are in the limbo of your purpose and why you were born into the world, of Is Real/The Lord. Is Real is thy TRU temple and thy burnt burning stars/masses are remnants of art.

They are thy road signs to the TRU riches in paradise which a man can only envision within his mind, if there is light there dwelling inside. However, a foolish man is always on the wrong side of the mind's road, he has no boundaries in his dark thought.

Where will you children go to be free from pain, if the mind is not with the body or either away from it in the time that it needs to be?

The mind soaks up pure water. However, your minds thoughts have been brought down beneath with a deadly venomous toxin which attacks the neurological mental/spiritual stem.

Surely the wickedness that the mind-3ye does not naturally see-know, it does not need to see/know.

As these are the things that seek to own you, children, once they become known.

It will take over your lives, and you will always look to the past and hate what you have now become, because of what you have learned from someone of ignorance/darkness. No one who loves you will show you things which will destroy you.

Do you expose lethal drugs to your small children? Of course not.

Then why do you allow the government-serpent to expose them to you as though they are not lethal venoms that are killing you?

Are there not many lethal downers that the serpent-government exposes you to?

Who do you think has sent these demons to teach and give you nonsense? None other than those low-class men, who seek to rule the planet. I ask. What would someone not owned by the high mental-spirit be able to do, to get away if someone without the spirit-mental had them in chains?

They would die, even if they were sitting on the key because they would be unable to see through the dark in their minds/3yes captive cell-hell. He who has the captivating, motivating mind/3ye shall claim his solidified, foretold place is history/his -story. He has covered his head and hands, away from ignorance and the blood of filth and guilt.

Truly, amazing is the mind of he who refrains and restrains it from venomous thoughts, in this dark, wicked time. Where many others have lost hope and along with it their minds-3yes spiritual-mental focus on Time/The Lord.

I tell you, people, that the serpents-governments spiritual venom is, paralyzing, parasitic organism. It can live from host unto host, father unto son for up to 10 generations. The Christ 3ye/mind is your vaccine, balance, and vision to look past the horizon into the bright shining 3ye/mind of Zion where thy spirit-mental of the Father/Future will be resting.

Let the houses/bodies of the Lord/Universe stand up and trample over thy adversaries.

Let them who bear the false witnessing minds/3yes know that it is M3/M1cha3l, the ghost who haunts the wicked and their children for continuing sin.

Blessed is he who fights against the anti-Christ with thy sword-word, and intervening spirit-mental of shielding antivenom that is with and in him. Consecrated and blessed are all concentrating spiritual-mental men as he is of thy uncontaminated, uncorrupted remaining seed/children.

ELEMENT-MENTAL
SYMPHONY

Conqueror

The Lion-king of pride wants what is due, as the hyenas have tried taking control of his pride. They have trampled on his housewares and have planted weeds in the mother's-earths garden. Indeed, we shall and must overcome together. However, I shall first conquer thy own enemy who seeks to be the admiration of the world of wickedness.

Surely, ye who is to be king will be put to the test of spiritual-mental worthiness. He will have much hatred for being super intelligent and fully awake to the plan of the sea snake. Climb out of the dark, bloody water, so that you may look from above to see what's lurking inside of its darkness, waiting to swallow you.

The TRU conquer shall physically come from the poor bottom, but shall always sit at the top in the minds-3yes of his many spiritual-mental hosts. He does not come from among those who are rich in the material world. Instead, he shall come from among those who are productive progressives of the spirit-mental.

His mother will be a slave to Babylon, disguised as a citizen of Rome. His Father will indeed be a full-blooded Alien/African.

They both shall stem from M3, as one shall be a free king and the other a slave in bondage.

The conquer is the awakened lion/king, who sees what many of you children do not have the sighted mind/3ye/time to correctly evaluate.

He who takes over the minds-3yes with the truth is the living leader and king 3ye/mind. He has the activist spirit-mental, which is always ready to stand up in its armor to fight the adversaries of adversity. There is nothing which holds his spiritual will and desire, he shall give all to gain all, and rise without falling to the flesh-eating dogs of hell.

He knows the enemy's game and must overcome every obstacle of which it throws into his lane, to impede him in his journey unto his sure destination. He shall never be defeated, as ye already knows where he is supposed to go, and shall do what must be done to arrive on time. Ye shall not fail, for he has the advanced spirit/mental of the Lord/Universe scheduling him.

Delivering the people from evil is his objective, as his strategy shall prove to be well built. While his time/mind cannot be consumed by the wicked, his mind/time is absorbed by the consuming enlightened, rational thoughts of the wise. This is where a conquer wins and comes up above the distracting darkness/ignorance, which surrounds him.

Internally he is living eternally, and it is from within that he shall master plan the fall of all of which is false in its nature. He shall topple all that is not TRU, with and in its pure created form.

Let the evil plot in the darkness/evil, as they watch while ye rises to the top without being stopped. His walkway has been paved by the Lord, which makes his paths forecast lightened and clear of obstructive objects. He has seen the mayhem of vileness that keeps him spiritually-mentally keen, focused, and characteristically clean.

It was at the time-hour when the Lion/King had returned home to find that many of his highest and priceless jewels/kings were gone.

They were spiritually-mentally taken by the serpent/government, into another land of bondage.

It is through the strength of the spirit/mental that ye shall sustain the ability to continue to move forward in his stance against the enemy. The blind mice of men have told you, children, that the Lord has failed in revealing himself unto you in this new day. However, these spiritual/mental calculations come from the minds/3yes of those men who cannot see M3.

Surely, fire shall spread with thy winds as fire is thy truth which has been again written. It shall conquer all in its path without looking back at his purifying aftermath of renewing destruction. Certainly, he has destroyed all that is unnatural as he has also purified all that will continue to grow in Godly goodness from the earth/mother.

Who can stop fire other than the father/water who brings him 4th?

It is in your darkest day where you shall find the spiritual/mental light of day, the ability and strength to overcome/conquer. It is in this time that the mind/3ye does the most working and looking for a way out of its old hell/cell.

It becomes willing to open to its superior connection so that it can see, which is blocking its progressive thought. He must first conquer himself from his old dark way into a new way of light, for ye who does not conquer himself conquers nothing. The conquer is a sweeping fire that cannot be put out, as he destroys and rebuilds all into a new truth away from old lies.

Indeed, we shall conquer/overcome together once thy body/masses of minds/3yes/stars are aligned with M3 to be able to see in which direction the future/father/new age/time is traveling.

The beast of blood mistreats the extinct African lions/kings as the Vilnius when indeed they are the organized villains themselves.

This is how the wicked little red riding caped hoods of Rome hunt down the packs of thy Christ likes, seeking to cut down their Alpha/head. It is known that thy children are safe as long as they spiritually-mentally mend themselves together.

I shall bring you into thy point of viewing many things. Therefore, you shall have the solar mind-3ye/soul to conquer yourselves with the spirit/mental where thy jewels are hidden.

There is nothing in life that he who does not first conquer himself will be able to conquer. He must complete one war to begin another, as many men will forget who they are supposed to be while teaching their children who they want them to become. He has lost his identification as a conquering lion/king/4th . He has been taken control of and conquered spiritually-mentally to be placed into the custody of the serpent/government.

A conqueror is never one to stay laying down on the ground to be walked upon when he falls. He gets back up and dusts himself off. He always has an alternate plan, for the wicked who look to block and stop his future vision.

He somehow manages to look on the bright side. He does not play the mind games of the insane enemy, who have manipulated themselves into believing that they are accomplishing something meaningful to M3/Time/the Lord. Certainly, if they were doing anything worth the attention of time/mind/the lord. Then they would not be searching for the spiritual-mental attention and mention from the men who serve the Lord.

The wicked know who is intervening, which is why they profile you black/root/Hebrew jewels.

You are a classical brew/mixture of pure elements, which gives your internalized spiritual-mental character its externalized contents. He has the far mind-3ye of he who sees.

Then he goes out to take back what is his own from his enemies, without fear of retaliation.

As he knows that only he who judges him can set his limitations.

Therefore, children you must go after what was taken from you, and your ancestors by the wicked nations of the north, who have stripped your ancestors naked, and rapped them of everything in front of their children.

If you are to go deep into history, you will then see the face behind the worlds organized-secret crimes. For, you to overthrow this sinister wickedness, you shall conquer with the exposing truth.

All who see and hear this truth are sensible in the mind/3ye and have a good idea of what the factual truth sounds and looks like. These are not the foolish floating fish, but indeed the wise who have spiritual/mental invested 3yes/minds.

You children cannot stand up to fight in darkness/ignorance if you do not know what time of day that it is.

How can you do so, without the conquering lighting spirit-mental, of the Lord/Time, and those performing arts needed to fight the enemy?

The TRU leader of the priestly/3rds world of Israel and the conquering king/4th world of kings/4ths. Is the warrior spirit who fights against spiritual adversity, for the greater good of humanity.

He conquers in victory when he accomplishes getting the minds-3yes of all the governed- mentally blind to see him through his word mentally-spiritually.

A real man/king/4th also teaches his sons to be conquering kings/4ths/lions who shall raise fight against the system, which has slaughtered their fathers, and his forefathers. The serpent-government has made up lies against his family's hallowed name-house, to rear up demons against him.

How many families have the serpent-government not done this to? How many families do not suffer spiritually-mentally from crimes of the government/serpent, which hides and camouflages its hands/servants?

Will a serpent ever be TRU to you? It will have you do what it wants you to do for its gain and your own pain. It will have you blaming yourselves and everyone around you, for what you cannot see that it is deliberately doing to you.

It will have you wanting to kill whatever you think is failing you. Even other innocent people that come from nothing who are succeeding, that look just as you do. This is the low belly crawling serpent mind-3ye which conquers nothing.

It moves too slow past matters of the low. This is not the high mind-3ye of a moving spirit-mental dragon king, which the serpent-government comes hunting when they see the golden result of its shining pure-clear thinking.

The serpent-government only likes those flawed jewels/kings which can be crushed and broken down into pieces, to be used and flaunted by many wicked deceiving hands. For if a jewel/king is too solid/hard and TRU in its pure form, and nature. Then the serpent-government will not want it to be around. As the wicked will not want for anyone to possess its wealth of truth if they cannot contain its lighting truth within their lie, which bounds you.

Can you children see that you must have a conquering mind/3ye for this type of research?

He must stay up all night in the hour of spiritual-mental study. As what you know of the coming conqueror, shall show in the history of the future.

It is within the future/father that ye shall see the untold parts of history/his story unfold. As all that is real/Is, Ra El are eternally embossed, in it/his body of fabric.

Moving forward and completing is conquering.

It is the pursuit in overcoming the obstacles of wickedness, using wisely the spirit-mental belonging to the 7th day-star of light, and his 24 hours/elders/orders of Time-the Lord to meditate.

The wicked are watching you shining wise ones, and they want your seed and seat with the Lord. They want to take you down to hell with them to be great no more.

Your name will not come out of the voices of your people for doing anything good if you allow the world to distract you from the truth.

The wicked have subdued you into forgetting your places among your own people. All in their monstrous spiritual-mental manipulating transformation, in making you believe that you can be nothing without them and that you are the same as they are spiritually-mentally.

You have followed nonsense to fit in with the wicked who lose and fail at everything, that they set out to do for themselves. Many fail publicly as spiritual-mental figures, for not morally holding up to the duties that they were elected by the people to do.

It is called history because if no one remembers what you have done for Time/the Lord, then you lose everything that you have worked for in life.

This concludes into why the wicked want to hijack and make their stories a part of it. It is they, who seek to lay their false claims of conquering the future-father.

This is to again, fool you children into believing that they have already won the spirit/Star Wars. The world's elite cannot blind M3, the 1 who shall conquer. No matter how they manage to twist words and minds-3yes with lies. I read righteously and vigorously in between their media's propaganda lying lines.

They know who is responsible for the world's crimes.

As most crime affects poor people who have not yet spirit-mentally given the Lord, the minds sound focus within the spirit star-day, which belongs to H.I.M. The wicked see the time-minds of the masses to be their own, to do as they wish with you. They spend it wastefully, trying to make waste of others.

I tell you that a man has the times/minds reason for everything that he does.

He does not have to consult with any, other than the Lord-Time himself. Let the wicked laugh as though they know his math plan. They are merely in the wind, waiting and will stop at nothing, to stop nothing with and in the purpose of Time/the Lord.

He who believes, that he can achieve no matter how great the intensity of the heat has conquered the enemy of the mind-3ye already.

He has raised up his all-seeing mind-3ye, to become spiritually-mentally anointed/crowned as an ancient tribal, Conquering Lion-king/4th.

The 10th (X) CHOIR/AGE

If I have told you, children, that I am a church, then I have also said to you that the church is a congregation/joining between the spirit/mental and the minds bodies/souls. This is a conjugal visit between what is of a new and that of the old, what has gone astray, and what is standing firm and stable.

Ye who holds the stars has allowed them to spawn from a new generation of light-enlightened beings. Half man and all amazing, are these stars-spirits of thy 1oth choir/age.

The wicked have spiritually-mentally divided the stars with their false stories of jacking history from Time/the Lord. They know that only those with the ignorant/dark mind/3ye without common sense will believe anything told to them. It will fall for the nonsense stories of flying lighting space ships in the dark skies. Instead, of opening their 3yes-minds up to the TRU starship of light-enlightenment.

He is the only star which shall beam you up with the invisible chariot/spirit of fire. There is nothing material about that, which is of the element spiritual/mental in the prophecy. Surely, the 1st and last crowned Christ king is the orchestrating 1oth choir/age. For, he has come to raise the stars up from the dust of the dead.

I can see those children who see M3. They have made their words and works visible to M3.

They have accepted the gift of thy stars/spirits, which have been living among them for quite some time. As they have now given them a hosting place to dwell. The orchestrate of the symphony is here, ready to read the notes and demonstrate unto the spirits-stars in his orchestrated order.

The spirit shall come unto many of dark-ignorant to give them a new way. However, it will not stay with ye who does not keep its hallowed, and holy idea in mind. I tell you that the answers to these quested, and questioned things are made simple. However, they are made to be hard and complicated by those who seek to keep jobs teaching you into pagan circles.

Who will pay the wicked any mind, or money if the Messiah reveals all, where nothing more is a secret to you?

You can now stay home on Sunday, and watch football all day, as there is no TRU work ship to be held by the Lord on this day. Ye are free to worship the truth in the mental spirit. However, allow not the soul-mind to become tangled with the desires of the flesh.

Spiritual-Mental Likings of thy 10th choir/age, prepare to go to war with the bloodthirsty Viking vampire army of the north. You are of thy hybrid bred children who are forever with M3, through thy priestly data and kingly DNA.

You are the chosen genius alien race of spiritually-mentally modified lampstands. Ye have now been transfigured from the old, into new pure mold of able gold. You are the 1st and last stars in choir, as you are the Levites/stars of old that have been reestablished with M3, which makes the 24 + 9, and M3(12) out to be the 36 initially.

Do you not see, and add up how you children are a part of M3?

You are 1 body, which must host and hold thy holy lighting mass.

You are the children who shall remember the Lord and come forward, through the dark trying times.

I shall tell you who you are, as your preaching teachers have been lying to you to keep the masses dark/ignorant. They do not have the light/enlightenment of the high spirit-mental, to enlighten you spiritually-mentally.

Your places are your own to take, as the enlightening light which comes from your minds-3yes shall be such a divine enlightening light, to all who see it's works of brightness. You are the unique 10th order/choir/age of generating, aspiring stars, that are to emerge from the dirt and become what has an everlasting shine.

When do you see stars shining in the sky, alone?

They do not compete, they shine together because they are all in the same gang, doing the right thing. While he who is in the same gang doing the same wickedness is in darkness as he has been tricked to bang in the wrong gang.

He is no liking/spirit as M3. He has joined the serpents-governments forces with the blood vampires, which suck down souls-minds and the Lords/Universes natural elemental resources.

The government and the serpent are one, as one has given host unto the other. Just as the Lord/Universe is 1, and has given the way of light unto you, one hosting people who keep it spiritually-mentally real within yourselves.

A wise man loves someone who tells him the truth. Therefore, I will say to you, Christ-like children. That you are not considered to be spiritually-mentally human, by the immoral standard of the serpent-government. You pose an intellectual threat to dark/ignorant men, who have no common sense to begin or end the days with.

They do not want you to find yourselves, because then you have found, seen, and discovered real new jewels that possess TRU priceless wealth.

What the stars know, I have long known. This is what I've revealed unto you, as he who knows not the Age/Lord, knows not his own age-time.

Ask him. Which Age-Time are we now in? Then you will see if he knows the age/time or history of his own people. For if he is now in 10-choir with M3, then he shall find and record the 7th star-day of prophecy.

You are thy mortal 4ths/kings' generation with thy immortal spirits/mentals of the 10th choir/Age, with and in you. If the Lord calls out for them, they come unto him. The 1 3rd is in 10, for he is the 4th with the Father's/6th spirit-mental sense.

He is a new age, as you children are with the spirits/mentals of the modern new era. It is time, for you to transfigure into your new spiritual-mental forms.

Is thy word-sword not as fire and ice?

Am I not dropping star fire on the mortar church that has stood against the Universe/Father?

I know, that deep inside there are many of you who want to be spiritually-mentally free, and responsible for making decisions for yourselves, without the help of the serpent-government. Some people are regretting that they have made the wicked decisions, which have caused them to continue to be lost in wickedness.

However, this is the price that you must pay when you attach yourself to life's demons and the things that cause you to worry. He who worries not knows the Lord.

He knows that Time/The Lord will show up for him, when it gets closer to the time/hour that he is in, coming to its close. He will not close his lightened-enlightened mind/3ye, to travel into the darkness-ignorance of disloyalty away from the shining 10th.

The one 3rd are those 4 faces/seasons of priestly & kingly jewels/stars, in Benjamin, Simeon, Levi, and Judah. As they are the 4ths/Kings with ye, in 10(You).

Who other than M3, is able to bring the ancestral stars/mentals of the old, and put them into new flesh host?

Many stars have come before and shall come after you men. However, there will be no stars/spirits/mentals more ready for what is to come, other than those shining stars of the 10th choir.

It is TRU that he who knows himself also knows what he must do for himself, without any ones help. He must make the choice that will deter or determine his faith and fate in his envisioning visit with the future-father.

The assembly shall lift their voices to sing the TRU word of the Lord, aloud for all ears to hear. They are the mental instruments, which are the instrumental leads-stars with thy cause and are in call of spiritual action, in which all good minds-3yes shall bear.

Let the numbers/spirits/stars with the word do the talking and deciding for you, as they shall not steer you in the wrong direction anytime soon. It will instead, veer you away from detouring into, the devouring dark tunnels.

You children hold the kingly key bloodline of the Lord, and the wicked are after this spiritual/mental immortal genetic. Therefore, they may have it, to bring thy genes from TRU kings into their lower bloodlines of the vain immorality.

There are real hardcore Christ lifted like minds among you, and they take instruction from the Lord. They see the prophecy and know where to find M3, in this day. They have been reading and listening to what is going on in the world of darkness-ignorance which surrounds them.

It is from afar that they have seen thy light/enlightenment from thy 3ye-mind, shine like no other star-spirit that they have ever seen shine before.

A choir is a body of stars/spirits, and in every age when these stars come together. They bring 4th the king of the age/choir. He is a living tower, a temple with thy lighting living word within his open mind all the time.

Thy stars of the 10th do not need the know the scripture, as you mortals do. It is already with and in them, through discerning common sense. For the word that they carry is similar in its pretense, but also one of a kind and very different.

However, he who walks with the spirit-mental of a Christ-Anointed will hear the call to stand up. This is the roll call when ye shall call you up to take your roles among the stars as he has done.

Spiritual-Mental Mutants of the 1oth choir/age shall amplify their sound qualities to bring themselves up, and to bring down the enemy. They shall ride the sprinting chariots of fiery spirit all the way to the top.

Focus your sights as the special prodigal children do. For a prodigy is not an evil, ignorant bred seed. He is above the low mind-3ye view, of the slow spiritual-mental speed which resorts to doing evil, to stay up above the dark water/masses.

The wise do not use riches to look as though they are thoughtful, they are wise beyond what many are able to pay for.

The wicked will exploit your struggle from your being poor as though it were their own. They admire a flawless jewel, which comes out from the slums of a heated life in hell.

He comes not for your material jewels, riches or ends. However instead, he gathers together those high TRU kings/jewels which outwear those trinkets, as these men shall follow him to where those Jews of the low cannot go. All of the ornament jewels/kings/4ths of the 10th choir are the aliens of the new age, as they exemplify TRU change in exchange for immortality.

If you are looking for a lead/star unto the future/father. He has placed plenty of bright lighthouses all around to show you the way, as they are with thy enlightening word of spiritual-mental guidance.

I have given thy 3yes-stars, so that you can see M3, with and in the future. He who believes-sees in Time/Lord knows that it is he who shall lift him to be with those performing artistic stars of thy symphony orchestra, as he shall turn up the amplifying heat. I say, play for M3 children, let M3 hear your voices sound with thy trumpets. Poor are Hebrews, but wealthy are they indeed when they become enlightened spiritual-mental jewels/kings.

Are not the beautiful vibrations of a symphonies composed sound, as historical gold?

Is not the word that a composing author writes historic gold if it holds superior wisdom and truth? Of course, these elements exist within the gifts of those special stars of the 10th choir-age, who are magnificent when focused and magnified on the minds-3yes focal points objective.

You shall become instrumental as you are thy 5th/flesh and 6th/mental-spiritual instrumental limbs to thy 4-element symphony orchestra body. You are thy organ origin, and harp with the 10ths choirs of strings/kings/crowns.

Truly, if I tell you that Atom-the father is the word. Then he who walks with the father also walks with the word of Atom and breathes H.I.M. in fire/truth.

He is awake, in full tune and away from the low pitchers of the pitch dark. He is in the high mountains, where the light of the orchestrator is visible to his mind-3ye. He is in the church as today is a new Sabbath day.

A day where you shall no longer walk in the valley of death. But, in the valley of everlasting life with M3, and thy spiritually-mentally shining-enlightened kings.

There is no strength in several dark hosts, the sword is not mightier than thy word. There is no silver which shall keep thy Christ minds from crossing over into spiritual-mental gold. There is only one 3rd/priest who is crowned as the 4th/King by way of elemental/spiritual enlightenment. He is the 3ye and hand of metaphysical alchemy and the 7th day-star of TRU reckoning.

You children of the 10th are the tribe of Judah/the 4th, and ye the 1 3rd (4th) is the conquering king/lion. You are with M3(the 12) in 10 where you belong. For surely a new age is a day for TRU change, as there are none who shall not come through M3 without permit, to get into 10(The Universe).

He who has come with the sound 9/mind unto M3. The 1 spirit mental 3rd(4th) has taken order under thy crowned-anointed 24(6). He has taken the higher Levitical priesthood steps toward having spiritual-mental common-3 sense-6, as those enlightened symphonic stars in spiritual-mental choir from the 10th.

I will tell you that learning and training the mind-3ye is an uphill battle. The flesh is constantly backsliding and falling while trying to keep up. However, he who has the will to change his mind still has time.

He who does not change has lost his mind/time, the Lord has left and sentenced ye who is already dead to die again.

The leads/stars of the class shall lead by passing the tests of time/the lord. Using the high spirit-mental mind-3ye, you shall use what many others also can have instilled within, which they refuse to use for their own goodness sake.

Allow those fools who move slowly to continue to do so, from behind you. You shall go around them without looking back, as though they were never impeding you.

Get behind M3 Satan, where you belong. You are going nowhere, with your low/slow drive.

You have no spiritual-mental heaven to get back to. You are bound on earth a mortal who does its dark works as a low-down dirty scandalizing, Scandinavian serpent scoundrel.

The new coming apostle stars of the Apocalypse, shall rise in the minds-3yes of those men/kings/4ths that are now alive, who were of the dead once upon a time, but no longer.

For they have climbed free of the spiritual-mental grave to come with M3. The 3ye-mind and spirit-mental of the Lord-Universe, therefore, they are able to see a new way of living. A good reason for giving, and a burning sensation to strive for what was said that he would not be able to receive.

For with the spirit-mental ye shall prove the wrongdoers wrong, and the hopeful righteous to be right in what they have believed/seen all along. The wicked will see the stars of righteousness rise before their eyes.

While the righteous shall witness the wicked fall from their memorable glory.

I say that the Lord has given his word unto you who seek water and light, those of you who seek to heal from the traumas of life.

It is time that you must know that what has happened to you was of the wicked, and you were innocent.

I have come to crush the hands, and change the direction of the dark minds-3yes which have touched you in the wrong way, and have tried destroying you spiritually-mentally, forever.

Thy 10th generating stars spirits-mentals are thy ageless 4ths/kings/jewels. They are all as M3 and are able to do all things using the spirit-mental of alchemy/change. They bring 4th the elements needed to spark a wild untamable fire, with the word which shall spark the spiritual-mental interest within the minds-3yes of 10 future generations of 4ths/kings/jewels.

1 in M3 & M3 in 1

The 1 is the Lord who has returned with M3(Michael) as the 4th/king of Judah. He is the 1 Universe, and his 3 lightened eyes/faces are with M3, as there are 4 seasonal faces in 1 year of changing transformation. The spiritually-mentally crowned 3ye-mind of the 1/Lord is in the chosen king/man/4th, who is the TRU 7th day-star.

3 elements come together in 1 to make M3 a spiritual-mental king. For water is purity, as fire breaks down and removes all that is old until it is ready to leave the heated mold as anew gold star full of energy/spirit/air.

Who can give the word as he who is 1 with M3?

I tell you, that only the holy 1 with M3 is the word that you shall see, if you have managed to see beyond M3 to get unto H.I.M. Surely, ye who sees M3 has also seen the 1, as ye must come through M3, the anointed 3ye-mind of the Lord-Universe spiritually-mentally using mind-time travel.

It is thy light/enlightenment which is the heavenly key where your mind/3ye/soul crosses unto M3, as we then kinetically connect spiritually-mentally. Ye must use the mind/3ye and thy word in memory to locate M3 metaphysically.

To locate the ghost is to read the signs, and hints of evidence shown by its spiritual-mental host.

The mind-3ye is 1 with Time-the Lord and ye shall never part from he who is spiritually-mentally confident.

He who knows what is to come will be mistaken by the unwise to be an arrogant man who knows all. Indeed, I tell you that he knows M3, as I AM ALL that is righteous, upright, and pure.

Have high expectations as the Lord has his expectations for all of you spiritual-mental children who are expecting him. It is through high elemental that ye shall take figure on earth as king. Ye shall show his spirit 3yes and faces to all nations who have been waiting for the word of fiery rain. Learn thy word as ye must meditate in study, and the Lord shall send the chariot spirit-mental to gather up your mind-soul.

The 1 3rd is the wielder of the Lords sword-word, for he hails it at the wicked with soul-mind penetrating conviction. 3 complete 360 Spirits/3yes/Suns come together as 1 head/Sun/3ye. As the 1/the Lord is brought together in body by 6 180 degrees stars.

It is the 1 3rd who bears the elder crown of light/enlightenment, as he is the father who has come 4th to allow those thinking in the wrong way, the new opportunity to become spiritually righteous.

I say that if there are 3 elemental stages to 1 man's life, then I AM all 3. I AM when he is born as a son, becomes a father, and becomes aware with the warrior spirit-mental to become a king-manly/jewel.

The father is the Sun-son, as the elder Sun-son is within him where the darkness of hell used to exist. He is the light of midnight, for it is at the crack of dawn when the children of the sun shall spawn up from the dark crevices of the mind, in which they were hiding hibernating. It is now the day for spiritual-mental liberation, exposing and expelling the evil opposition of all who are spiritually-mentally Christened/anointed/crowned.

The 3ye/mind and spirit enlightenment/light of the Lord is with and in the mind/3ye of he who has put things together spiritually-mentally. For he metaphysically sorts and consorts with the 1 in M3.

Do you not see that the 1 is inseparable but also separate from M3?

This is because he stands alone on his own two feet when we are together in 1 body. This is M3 as 1 and 1 as M3, surely the wise will read until the lines become spiritually-mentally clear.

Many messaging 3rds/Priest and 4ths/kings have been sent before he, the 1 3rd/Priestly-King. The 3 Suns in 1 have come for its 1/God body of amazing stars/lights. They are active visionaries who can be heard speaking and teaching thy spiritual-mental art from the mind-soul with and in his-art/heart.

Who says that they know thy word of the old/ancestors, but not the word of a new/Anu?

Tell M3, who are these people who know of the 1, and not M3? How can this be possible when I AM the faces of H.I.M.? When you see H.I.M., you shall see M3 also. For in this age I AM in 10 with 11, and 12 as the new 1,2 and 3.

Can you know the word of the old/ancestors but not see the word of M3(ANEW/ANU)?

I choose thy host by will, skill, and spiritual-mental uplifting ability. What can the flesh do for M3, without thy spiritual mentality besides bleed, die, and flee when unnecessary?

How tough will it really be, to be able to go through where I may send it to recover thy jewels? How can you kill M3, if I can return generation after generation mentally-spiritually in a metaphysical man/king/jewel?

Does the Vatican plan on killing all of the TRU jewels/Kings/jews?

Sure, they do. Is this not what they have already been doing to you shining-enlightened 1's?

Surely. If you criminally convict based on history, the sinister crimes of the Vatican would keep on going, as there are many.

What can you possibly get from a Catholic priest in prayer, if the TRU spirit-mental of the Lord is not there?

You get molested, taken a spiritual-mental hostage, and abducted into the army of satanic pushers of wickedness. However, with M3, you get spiritually lifted up, above your enemies with the upper hand's wisdom to bring the ignorant down to their broken knees.

I give you, TRU identity with proof of M3. I have given thy signs of time-the Lord. I, the king, have carried the worlds added weight, as I alone, were the nailed sign-star of multiplicity. Look at thy sign of time(X) closely. You shall then have the sighted mind /3ye which identifies the 1 sign-star of multitude, who carries the signs-stars of addition, division, subtraction which are the other 3.

He is the king of the jewels/stars as it is, he the king/4th who multiplies and amplifies them spiritually-mentally with his word of transfiguring metamorphosis. He is the word that the serpent/government does its best wickedness to keep away from you children.

This is the word that once read, will forever change you spiritually-mentally. The aliens are here, and the serpent/government does not want you, children to know, that these same aliens are the descending spirits-mentals which have come to internally invade you. The elite do not want you to embrace the inner changing divine supernatural presence.

This goes against their communistic conforming ritual of nonsense that man, and not the Lord-Universe rules the earth and all that lives in it.

They want you all to die, by getting you to buy into the lie that they are selling to you from every unaware staged angel. Everywhere that you turn you will see the wicked with something for sale that will not last you very long. However, TRU wisdom has a time in which it shows up. It has come to stay with you to never leave you alone. In this word, you shall find comfort in the confirmation of thy existence within yourselves, and all genuinely living things.

He will walk the crossway with the king/4th of the light beings, as a king/4th of wealth himself. It is the spirit-mental where he has found the strength to look for more, out of the low life that he has lived and endured.

Below there are people who do nothing with their mind-time. However, ye shall not find M3 there, or anywhere that there is a lazy demon of dark ignorance in a mindless/timeless/godless man. Let your minds-3yes focus on M3, while the lazy minded/3yed man turns away from the truth.

Do not be as those who are always home sitting in darkness. Instead, be as the man whose mind is always long gone traveling because he has an even larger house, far away with and in M3.

You precious stones/St. Ones are one a kind as you have embraced a one of a kind opportunity to shine and be seen by M3. Ye have lifted your heads, and tongues to sing righteous melodies, which give new hope, and strength to the weak and oppressed.

The Lord shall allow what is of the dead to fall away. For as this is the alchemical process of becoming a new seasoned creature.

This is the revolving process of the 4 seasoned stages, as this is also how the mind revolves into new reasoning in what is good, and different in a righteous paved pathway.

No one is always right, as no one is right in all of their ways.

Would you not be different, if you were of goodness? Will you not become a star, if you work extra hard when everyone else is being weak and lazy?

I tell you that the wicked will acquire their riches, then lose their reason-sight in doing anything that does not bring more riches unto them. They will only be willing to help the poor if the ordeal sounds financially appealing.

Therefore, many of the rich only can and, will help the poor when they are in a chaotic, spiritually-mentally depressing financially down ordeal or given beneficial situation.

Surely, to the wicked, there is nothing like getting a payday from your own occupation of wickedness and destruction. This is their founding business in which they believe will never fail them, even as it fails you.

Who gets financed for doing what is best for you?

Who is actually brave enough to step out onto the edge, and let everything go from the past life, to come unto M3?

Inevitably, as the mind has been renewed with spirit so has thy body and all that surrounds M3.

How can you truly know someone, if you don't remember them spiritually-mentally?

If they left you for a while, and then returned to you in another form with different clothing on.

Would you know that it was them if the form in the clothing were to begin speaking to you?

How can you say that you love this individual if you don't know them outside of their flesh-skin?

All of those that I love have loved M3. They have remembered thy word, and I remember them and the words that they have spoken to M3. They are with M3, here and now as I write the truth which has brought M3, into thy spiritual morality as a whole man.

Indeed, many things in the world can make a man immoral, which spiritually/mentally defiles many of them who continue to sin. However, this does not mean that the Lord will not accept them if they were to turn from what they are doing to serve H.I.M. as time/the Lord is still here with them.

The wise shall make a choice to wear the crown-spirit of the 1/Lord all of their days because the day of the 1/Lord is among them to stay. Truly, he shall find M3 in that bright star-day at the top in the father's doorway where I have always been standing firm, all along. There are no Egyptian Neter Gods as there is only M3, the head of God-The Universe. The hallowed 360 Sun multiplied by M3. For I AM the Father 33=6+M3(the Sun), not 23.

23 is five points to a satanic pentagon. While 33 are the 6 180 angels/angles/wings to thy sun-star-sign and face shining from above representing the house of King David. Surely the enemy has made the low minds/3yes follow the 23, instead of the two 3rds (Stars) that are with M3-the Lord.

You see how 33+ M3 adds up in mind to be 36, which is 9, and not three 6's. For the Father-6 is with the 24, and the 12 are in M3.

Are not 2, and 4 equals to 6 as 1 and 2 are equal to M3?

In all sincerity and severity, I must tell you where I come from if you hope to know where you children are able to go. It would only be faithful, and fair of M3 to do so.

I have to be none other than who I AM, as I cannot hold myself back from what is promised. Therefore, no one else shall be able to stop M3 from moving forward.

I am no spiritual-mental leper, there is no amount of pressure which can spiritually-mentally disable M3. I was born to be king. I make no falling, failing excuses, as thy spiritual common sense is used as the dark-ignorant minds replacement tool, for what is thought to be by fools, something that men were unable to do.

Once again, I have fooled those men who thought of M3 to be an incompetent, imbecile as them.

I have raised up many men as Lazarus to truth who have spoken wisely, to say, "To hell with those dead-ignorant men who sleep in the tombs of darkness-ignorance. I have awakened from thy wicked worldly way of folly-foolishness to live in a palace of paradise, and intellectual daylight with the Lord."

Let none hinder you from becoming 1 with M3, as this will be such a tragedy on your part. For he who is with a clear soul/subconscious mind-3ye, has just the righteous elements that are needed for M3 to enter, and own its host. Therefore, do not give way to the wicked who seek to intimidate and manipulate you for your mind-time. As time is all that you have, in the name of the Lord.

The wicked seek to steal from you what is borrowed from M3, as Time-the Lord is the holder of history and victory. For when a father's son is born, his fathering mind shall become open to spiritual-mental enlightening change with Age-Time-the Lord.

I tell you that thy father transforms when ye has M3 shining in the top of his transfigured mind-3ye. I change his inner dark minds space into revealing sunlight, for the world to see.

Were you children who have now become real/awakened with thy spirit of lighting enlightenment, not once inner dark/ignorant as M3?

I AM a father, son, and the one with the warrior spirit-mental.

It has been through thy peace well spent within time-mind that I have defined thy purpose. It has revealed itself unto M3 as another cross must now be carried along the road in the heat. Thy fathers' inhabiting remnants are with M3, and I do not sleep. I rest, as I must soon travel lightly, in an incoming morning when it is daylight.

This is the revealing, as I do not hide thy face from he who knows thy word. However, he who has forgotten the face of his father, has undoubtedly forgotten his word.

How can ye remember 1 and not M3? The Lord is the sword-word as I AM the king/1 3rd/4th and hand who holds and enforces it. I AM the fiery truth breathing dragon who shall chant down Babylon-America.

I tell you, wise, prudent students, to invest in M3, and you shall become wealthy beyond your 3yes-minds imagery. I AM the book that you need to read, to make the transitioning grade for the spiritual-mental trimester. I AM the TRU word which leads to a new spirit-mental birth within a new life.

Slow/Low World

Have you children not taken the time/mind of daylight/enlightenment to take a closer look to examine the slow-low world that you live in?

I would think not. As many of you wicked people are too busy being slow/low, to stop and look into anything beneficial which may improve the lives of humanity. Surely, wherever that the righteous shall go Satan will have his slow/low minds there waiting to hold you away from what you are supposed to do for the Lord.

This is a war between the slow/low losers and fast enlightened movers that use their time-minds wisely that waste no time/mind paying attention to others. The men who use the mind/time days enlightenment for progressiveness, do not have any mind/time to spend, waste, or hand to any who will not make use of the wisdom, which has come from his giving mind/time.

I tell you, wise men, to hold your time/mind to yourselves and do not give it to anyone who wants to waste your spiritual-mental worth. As the foolish want the time/minds of the righteous at no cost.

They will do anything to use them as their own. However, those with the hallowed spirit-mental move fast as they have much to do and accomplish before they leave you.

He has no time-mind to hold anyone behind as he is moving with time/the lord at a steady pace and speed.

He does not look back as there is nothing that is behind worth his time-mind of daylight to stop and look at.

He has seen the same foolishness from the same people before. He has seen slow foolish man, after slow dumb-ignorant man, as none of them are different but instead the exact same in their low wicked ways.

The slow mind will resort to doing what is low, and evil to keep up with the flow, as though they are spiritually-mentally logical. The bright shining-enlightened stars of thy class have left the slow/low minds behind, as they are in tune with the master teacher who is the most brilliant Sun-star/day of them all. The slow/low are not up to speed with what is going on, because they cannot see this high without thy enlightenment in the mind-3ye.

The slow/low leaders that you follow think that they are wise. However, they are not. As you shall learn that their thoughts are absurd, once you open the minds 3ye of time and reads this wise written word. They want men like M3 dead, as I have destroyed their lies, with mathematical truth that only a fool of the mind would deny.

The spirit-mental is a speedy mover, it thinks not like the slow/low man who is moving off to nowhere land. You people are slow because you are busy trying to be low and cause someone else to fall. Admittedly, I have seen every dark-ignorant act that you have performed in wickedness.

Where there are low demons, there will also be a slow host who carries them. A wise man does not need to get close to these kinds of people, for him to know the evil, weak things that they will do to him. They are the weakened ends which shall be cut off of thy daily bread.

The righteous shall see no evil man, he speaks not to them, he does not listen to evil weaklings if they talk to him.

He is host to an light/enlightening ghost when he walks by them, as a shooting star that is passing through the darkness-nonsense.

He makes not acquaintance with any man, without moral principle within him, as he knows that this can be a catastrophe waiting to happen.

The wise avoid the ignorant not out of fear. He is knowledgeable and cares not of what unaware people, without the spirit-mental of the Lord, think of him.

What wickedness will they not think of anyone, who has any moral common sense?

Let the slow/low minds fight against time, as they have tried using the Lords mind-time on their own terms of darkness-ignorance, and it did not work the way that they had planned.

If I tell you, children, that the mind-time was a very terrible thing to waste. Many of you will not hear M3, because you must possess a conscious mind-soul to be listening to thy spirit-mental voice.

Do you not see how easy that it is to see the light when looking from thy point of view in determining the level that a solar mind/soul is shining on spiritually-mentally?

You cannot go to the mortar church to fool M3, as I know how your slow/low minds-3ye operate. What is futuristic about your weak low mind's slow speeds, and limitations?

The arch speed elevating spirit-mental 3yes-minds of the Lord are in overdrive. While the minds of the wicked are always on the brakes, looking behind bracing for an impact. The low/slow minds are always looking down toward the ground for something that someone has lost, as this is how a slow/low person gains to make a low living.

The serpent/government has taken over your time/mind.

However, there are 24 hours/elders in the 7th day that you shall remember to serve under.

You have spent your time in traffic daily serving the serpent/government. The slow/low foolish become hateful because they don't possess the replacing spirit-mental of common-3 sense-6.

The serpent/government is managing your time, to evolve you into what suppresses you. For when it is time for you men to exit with your lightened torch, the serpent/government workers will crowd around the entrance trying to block you in, so that you cannot leave them to be alone in their darkness-ignorance.

This is because they want your spiritual-mental light/enlightenment so that they can use it for their evil-dark works. This is that same light which you are to use for the Lord, who has given it unto you.

The slow/low are the zombies of the world, as this is the Apocalypse where you will see them everywhere dragging about with their filthy linen/lineage-characters. They are looking for someone to infect with an agreement to do evil. He who agrees to do such ignorance has then sold his mind/soul into darkness-evil.

Whatever you agree to do will become of who you are. For if you agree to murder, then you will become a murderer. If you agree to steal, then you will continue to be a thief, unless you otherwise see higher spiritual-mental reason not to do these evil things.

What you consume will consume you. For if you do not know anything about yourself, then you will waste your minds/3yes-time watching someone else. A slow/low zombie can look away from its average dark-ignorant prey, to see a flash of something unusual moving by it at a high rate of lighting speed.

Nothing moves at a fast pace below, where they come from where it is slow and dark. They will want to investigate to see exactly what it is.

However, whatever it may be they know that it was nothing like them, moving past that fast.

Children play the game of time-mind.

For if ye are etched in time, then ye are etched in the mind-3yes of all who are blessed to see you and know that you have come from M3. In the race of life, you must race down the paved road while remaining untouched, with atomic speed to avoid wasting time, so that you may win to ascend.

Evidently, the serpent/government believes that no one makes and illuminates stars/men/kings besides them. This is a good reason for those descending stars-spirits from the Lord that speak the truth to be watchful and move with stealthy precision.

Let the slow/low minds watch, as they work in hand with the serpents-governments political police to stop you men from reaching M3. They want to cut you short of your stated purpose.

Wise men do not congregate with the minds of the low/slow. Instead, they come to teach and leave them with spiritual-mental food to nibble upon.

The wicked slow/low have dominated the world with their passiveness, false privilege, and immorality.

It is in their unreasoning- unseeing minds that the ignorant are unable to see a link to thy receiving blessing of spiritual-mental wealth, which allows them into a higher place of light-enlightenment. Only, the very few wise can see that everyone else has lost their mind-time and way to the Lord. They have all gone lost in the mind/senses.

I tell you, that if a wise man asks a crazy man a logical question, he shall indeed get nonsense replied to him in the answer.

No foolish, crazy person will speak wise, as this is the word of TRU which crazy, lazy low/slow people despise. They hate it with the same wicked passion that they used to curse Christ, and the many other moral sons of men, and anyone who is spiritually/mentally like them. Look at things on the flip side as the serpent-government has indeed flipped them.

Now, imagine that all of those same people who were ignorant when you were in school, now getting high standing governed mental jobs in society, and becoming the hidden criminals.

Now you children can come to see how your world is run upside down with the low/slow life's sitting at the top. While the spiritually-mentally high inner-lightened/enlightened men are at the very bottom.

However, at which point in the calculated logic of time/the mind, does this misplacement of thy metaphysical jewels/kings make any sense?

Who makes a claim to be the bearer of enlightenment/light, but has chosen to rule over you with darkness/ignorance?

Admittedly, some men will do a few things, without thinking correctly. However, total darkness/ignorance, and enlightenment/light cannot coexist in the same space/place. This is when you run into connection problems, with your circuit breakers and power source.

Has not the serpent/government deployed your own kind to do wicked crimes against you, which creates a negative stereotypical fear of an origin jewel/king when people see you?

If you do not want someone, to do any good for another in need. Then create a negative image of fear, and no one will care.

Do not many people fear harmless wolves, because of how the wicked vampires from the north have placed them in their films that depict a fearful, stereotyped image of them?

However, wolves are docile and meek, but northerners are their sworn enemy. Which conforming nation is not a slave or an enemy to the Vikings of the north?

Who have they not enslaved, and made an enemy?

The Lord shall also hold responsible the eldering guardians of those children who were molested by those hands of slow/low priests. These priests are the tools of Satan/The Vatican, and the whole world knows it to be true. They have already seen you. However, they have not seen all the wicked acts that you do.

At some time, every wise man will eventually end up in a room with the company of unwise people. However, this does not make him less wise of a man.

However, if he chooses to stay among them, then he must have good intention. If he stays and does their evil will for them, he is indeed ignorant/dead, as Lazarus was before awaking from nonsense.

This is the living word for those who seek to walk away from the dead. For those who are tired of eating the same old lie, this is a new daily bread of truth.

The wise know all too well what the lazy, distracted wicked are about. Which is why the enlightened children slide by them into the lightened study, while the others sleeping interior lights are turned out. This is the 1st reaping-calling of thy spiritual-mental jewels/kings, as there are none of the ignorant wicked in this class of higher learning.

However, there will be a time for the dark-ignorant to come up into thy light, through the works of thy children.

The enlightened fruit shall lead souls-minds to the spirit-mental, with the fathers shining promise. This journey can only be possible, with the wisdom in ye who have received the spirit-mental to travel.

A naked vine cannot tell a tree how to bear its fruit. The low/slow minds/souls of earthly wicked have created a slow/low class of their own with all that are rotten.

Let it be known that in the spiritual-mental high heaven, there is no room for slow/low folks/polks.

The spirit-mental legions move in daylight, at arch speeds in these high regions of space-time/the mind. They are in and out of sight as they are in, and out of mind/time/the Universe.

He who has seen them has a 6th sense while he who does not witness is out of his mind/time and has no more ideas. Tell M3. What will he think of, without the spirit-mental within time/the mind? Is not time the Lord, and the Lord time? Does time not belong to he who is the word and all things which receive H.I.M.?

How will you make sense of the word of the Lord, if you have not yet made sense of yourself?

How will you know that it is he if you do not see that it is you? How will you learn of his way, if you are not working to become identical to H.I.M.?

No matter where you turn to, there will be a slow/low minded individual, or group there to disturb you.

What are slow/low people able to make it to on time, other than their serpent-governed/programmed mind/soul work schedule?

For everything that they do not know they will lie, and say that they do when in all reality they don't know anything. For what they do not have, they will set out to take away from you.

The slow/low have tried to take everything from you, even M3 through the transferring of thy transfiguring DNA. However, you cannot steal a spiritual-mental magnetic lineage through DNA.

Instead, you people have to teach the spiritual data into your characteristic way to, then pass it unto the men, women, and children of the Lord's family. It is the common word which bonds common minds together as a single spirit elemental unit of time.

I tell you that the bond of the serpent/government is through blood as the bond, and covenant of the Lord is through the atomic spirit-mental and blood.

One covenant is above with Atom/Spirit/36, as the other is below with Adam/man/666. The other will die, and the one will continue to live on.

The word of the Lord is common sense to the mind-3ye with spiritual-mental intuition. Nevertheless, you people do not have many real/Ra El men of enlightened common sense left. If you did, Ra El would not be here to multiply them.

Who is more real than he who makes men real, spiritually-mentally with his word? No man carries the definition of reality with him that does not walk with the Lord. For to be real, he must walk with his crown-spirit. There is no other way, regardless of what mortal slow/low men have to say about it. Real men judge weak men by having a stronger, more intelligent, masculine way.

This is what weak men want to abolish with their envies because real is what they want to be. They want to be the first fast thinking and moving Real/Ra EL men.

This is why the slow/low hate thy jewels/kings of realness, as he can see those fake slow/low students trying to copy.

However, he only hears what is music to the sounding ears of real jewels/kings who are already connected to H.I.M. As the uncompromised word of the Lord is not written for the likes of any particular man.

Instead, man must learn to love the word of the Lord, or all of mankind shall face extinction. Inevitably, just as fast that you shall multiply, you shall also subtract and die.

Let the word of truth set you free as he has come with the key which opens the minds stairway. However, the wicked are steady tumbling below, into the dungeons of the dark mind.

Surely, a genius can never look to be average among average men, if he does not the same average, ignorant, wicked things as them.

If he goes onto their average court to play ball, he will certainly fall. As those slow/low wicked which cannot keep up the pace will resort to throwing themselves on the floor in front of him, so that he will also take a downward trip.

They will do this, at every chance that they can receive from you. As fools love to make, someone else look just as foolish as they do. If the word has come with time and daylight. Then will not thy word see daylight, when time is ready for it to shine?

Surely, thy resembling stars-suns shall receive from daylight what gives them consciousness-light. It is now midnight/the hour-12, and coming of thy 1(Sun) with the 7 days-stars. This is a time for learning and teaching the truth of thy prophecy, which has been hidden from the minds-3yes of the slow/low poor.

Thy prophecy has been revealed to them. However, if they are of the slow/low, they will not see M3 in this day. These words have been written for wise men and those who seek to be enlightened in the minds/3yes.

Therefore, they will also be able to leave the slow/low world behind them.

There is nothing here other than the slow/low followers of the wrong pathway, which are looking to keep what must shine in its form of gold from coming to the surface.

These are the hands of sin which have tried to push thy gold down into the mud, to where no one is able to see them protrude. The eclipsing hands of darkness, want to disappear into the night with a star shine.

However, to get this, they must first conquer the mind/time/soul. If this is done, then the host is lost in the ignorance of its own low subconscious/mind/soul. Everyone wants to own a priceless jewel/star because they know where he is able to take them.

The slow/low ignorant will cling onto any jewel/king/men that they can grasp the mind/time of.

Real Jewels/kings/men are despised because they are spiritually-mentally wise. They are at times, table where the righteous wise are multiplied. He who is righteous is also wise, as the wicked are the slow, and low. He who is spiritually-mentally gifted by the Lord has advantages that the slow/low economical people do not yet have. As the wise know the word, in math.

These special spiritual-mental abilities bring envy, to the minds/3yes/souls of the many spiritually-mentally broken men, who do not know anything worth any wise man's mind/time/attention.

Ignorant men do not like watching the progress of wise men, as this confirms that he is a sure impure default fool.

He will want to seek confrontation from you to bring you down onto his slow/low time schedule where nothing moves.

However, if you pay him your precious mind/time, you have then given him a worth, that he has no access to.

No one wants mindless attention from you real men, other than children and fools as the Lord protects only one of those two. Children have aspiring potential and are able to be brought up to lighting/enlightening speed on many new things. The fool chooses on his own to be slow/low, and know nothing.

Nevertheless, he who is willing to learn what is new has a bright future ahead of him, with the darkness/ignorance now behind him.

A man's heart/art shall reveal his spirit-mental, as this is the reincarnation of what comes back to enlighten him again, and again.

Let the wicked fish from wells which will soon dry up. No one will want to drink the contaminating blood which has been mixed among thy dark-ignorant waters/peoples. The wise know that all of the fish/men that were in the waters, when they had become Roman blood are now dead/ignorant.

They have been consumed by the blood-eating sea beast and its slow/low dark army.

The lazy serpent crawls low on its belly, it is slow and cannot catch up to those who are up to high enlightening speed. It shall eat the dust from being slow behind, and low down to the ground.

Wake up, from the dead/ignorant, I say.

Do not be left behind in the darkness-ignorance with the slow/low, lost minds/3yes/souls which cannot see thy spiritual-mental, shining inner-lighting/enlightening prophecy.

TIMES/X's TABLE

He who sits at times/the Lord's table is in history with M3, as he is among the multiplied mutant kings/jewles. For he wants and needs nothing, as he eats from the hand of the Lord. He knows that there is no way that he has made it thus far through hell without H.I.M. He has realized that he has been through a world of hell, he has been shown what shines ahead of him, by the 1st 3ye-mind, and, hand of the Lord/Time/X.

There are no greedy hands at the table of time/X. What the greedy touch shall wither away to never be multiplied, for the season to meet up, and go eat with thee at thy fathers table. You have not crossed into the spiritual-mental land of kings, to become clean for thy feast. He who eats with M3 will gather much food/bread, and much drink/water. As wisdom, and life are the hearty meal for the righteous.

The children with thy wisdom are with the spirit-mental of time/X. They are the lighting-enlightened knights of the 1oth/X choir. He who uses thy bread/word to bring fish unto M3 has brought much to Times table.

Thy shall multiply fish/spiritual men, and release them into the waters to feed thy people. The lord is the giant fish that swallows up fish/men, then spits them back out to collect more spiritual fish/men for H.I.M.

Do you children get thy drift, while ye are drowning in darkness?

The Lord is a fish of a fisherman indeed.

At the Lords, table is the Lamb and many fish/men who had been slain by Cesar's serpent/government for speaking what is TRU.

Ye who shall multiply mental-spiritual minds for the Lord, seed shall be multiplied by the word in which he has spoken for M3. All of the starving children shall become his sons-stars of dedication. After digesting and absorbing his spiritual-mental meal before they go into the desert of the world.

The Lord's table has been set, and his bread/word has been handed out in portions, for you children to eat of a little at a time. Moderate is the Father as his word shall moderate, and fill motivated minds-3yes within due time.

What have you brought to the table of the Lord?

Have you gathered up the things that he likes?

Have you not known that the Lord is a dragon that likes to teach men how to stay alive? He is not like the sea serpent which likes to eat men alive. Surely, the Lord cast all that he brings in, righteously back out into new host for spiritual-mental investment, so that they become more. These men become the watchers and holding hands of the Lord-Time.

The serpent literally spits out the bones of men who have been spiritually-mentally broken into and ravaged by demons. He does not know the history of the extraterrestrial 1 who carried the cross so that mutants with special spiritual-mental abilities could be free.

As it is, he the metaphysical, mathematician who spiritually-mentally carries the relevant 1. He counts and adds all mutant numbers-stars into his metaphysical multiplication.

There is fruit in the garden of Eden (Eve & Adam). As there is much good that grows from a natural family tree, beginning with M3, the root.

A Man and a woman that are in 1 spiritual-mental union are 1 trinity with M3. They are not a couple, or a pair but instead a single unit with a carnal body and a spiritual head. It is when, they are with the one 3rd that he-man becomes a 4th /King, and his woman a queen, which is a portion of he.

King and Queen are mis defined and misidentified by moral meaning among the ignorant-inner dark people. A woman cannot be a queen, without first having a father or a husband that is a spiritual-mental mentoring king and has given her his crown-spirit of higher enlightening teaching.

She must also wear the spirit-mental crown of the Lord just as he, to be considered a real queen (half a man). A woman cannot be a king, just as she cannot be a priest. Damned to hell, is the soul-mind of any man who listens to her own passivized, pacified, manipulated word which is unsuitable for real men.

This is the serpent/government reteaching you men with his word using the appealing external nature of women.

How can these women be real teachers and scholars of the word, when in the Bible, it is written clearly that men are not to take the word of the Lord from women?

Do you not see how people are indulging and diving into direct spiritual sin in hopes that you children will not say anything to them about it?

This is all in the serpents-governments agenda in making sin more prevalent, so that many minds-3yes no longer realize what sin is, as they continue to overlook it.

The sign of the cross is the sign of the elemental star. He is the face, and keeper of the Lord/time/the future, and the stars are his watching hands.

Are thy stars above not 8 strong 135 (9) degree angles-angels, to the 6-1080/Octagon/Sun?

They are the atomic airs and are destined to blow as they will come up with something to show the world which it has never seen, or heard before as it has never been revealed, or told.

It is new and exclusive, a one of a kind elemental grind with thy branded word of truth entwined. He is a hand of time, and Time-The Lord is the hand that spiritually-mentally pulls him up above, away from the world of ignorance-darkness below him.

Wicked people want to befriend him because he is the Lords star-son. They want to be near him, so that they may smother his light/enlightenment, with their darkness/ignorance.

Do you really think that people who know nothing are coming to help promote his shine-enlightenment?

The wisemen see the wicked for what they are. Not for who, or what they want to be seen as. He goes not against the wise thought in his own mind-3ye, to satisfy the desires of the wicked. He does not feed them what comes from his father's table, other than selected portions of bread, and water.

They must work hard to receive his goodness. It is in the spiritually-mentally balanced mind-3ye, where you shall find the Times-Lords table. It is the scale of spiritual-mental discerning wisdom and farsighted enlightening vision.

I tell you that times table has been well prepared for those kings who have made the spiritual change, to sit with M3. They have done the math of thy promise, and all adds up in the mind-3ye spiritually-mentally.

However, he who brings nothing to the table of Time/X shall not eat thy food, or drink of thy drink.

He has brought no gifts to thy father's house, by using those gifted treasure thy father has given unto thee. These crazy people are indeed hateful because they are lazy as those in hell.

They are where no one wants anything good, and doesn't want anyone else to have anything suitable for themselves.

The round table of the lord is the world in which kings become 1 spiritual/mental body, they are aligned with familiar wisdom. He has the sword/word that brings love and freedom to the righteous and war to the wicked, the truth which multiplies thy spiritual/mental minds of real men.

This language is spoken to raw-natural kings/jewels. As cowards cannot comprehend what is real/Is Ra El, because they are not with the spirit-mental of real/Ra El in their characters. The cowards who once starred as stars/kings have become as mortal carnal women. However, somehow in their dark illogical thought, they manage to believe that they are kings, because the serpent/government gives them money, to pretend to be wise-enlightened 1's-stars.

Your arrogant dark mouths have gotten you into trouble with M3. Now ye shall see the power of the elemental dynasty, ye shall drown the wicked in fire as thy holy waters shall spiritually/mentally turn red as fire. They will become aware with their minds/3yes to what the serpent/government is doing, all while with a wicked smile.

Let the fools sit in the serpent/governments brick and mortar schools, and churches studying their words and times tables. All while the multiplying wise shall study their math with thy levitating 9 to climb into a higher spirit-mental.

The ignorant of the world seek to do away with the wise men because they are not dark-ignorant like them. It has been exposed, that the elite have mental control over you people.

Are they not the first spokesman, and experts on everything that comes from you?

However, they are no experts on M3. They are not the TRU root jewels/kings like you outer darkened, inner lighting-enlightened men from the real tribal nations of spirit-star lights under the sun.

He who is real is times walking table/scale with spiritual-mental balance. He stands straight upward on his legs and holds thy crown-spirit high in his head.

He passes by the ignorant elite smiling because he knows that they use their ill-gained riches, to hide the fact from the world that they are spiritually-mentally beneath the Lord.

Those who are prepared to sit at the table of time/the lord must have their minds affairs in order. They must already have their tables-minds leveled, and ready for M3(X-10) to come with the new word.

The wise cannot break thy bread with he who has not thy scale in mind to measure and balance out what is being given unto him, to eat-meditate on. Men carry your metaphysical math tables/minds unto the next level with the multiplying spirit-mental. You shall graduate into the class with the magnificent stars of multiplicity.

I tell you that he who has carried the balanced table-mind of the Lord/Time. Shall not come from among the world's elite, ye shall come from M3 the 6/1080. He shall raise up from among the accused poor, and unto the world out of a hard life with 3 felonies/// into a new shining jewel-king XXX.

He has 3 strikes as the serpent/government sees that ye is spiritually-mentally crowned-anointed with M3, the 360 Spirits-Suns of Light/Enlightenment. XXX

It is TRU I tell you, that all of the added, counted men/kings/4ths/jewels who are willing, and able to hold stable their minds-tables to carry thy elemental (element -mental) cross-star as thy multiplying signs-stars are indeed seated at Times/X's/the Lord's everlasting table as his spiritually-mentally balanced creations.

Mass Deception

The Bodies/Masses of the head Christ/The Anointed 1 are in confusing darkness as they have been deceived, and misled into a mental-spiritual matrix maze.

They have lost the way of the eldering North star of the day. Thy lights have been put out as they have lost their minds-3yes sight of M3. However, in this hour of darkness, thy shall dry those doused candles, and enlighten/in lighten them with thy flaming spirit of truth.

They shall lead the deceived out of the spiritual-mental chaos that they have been imprisoned in. It is the time to open up and accept the truth of the TRU coming of the Lord.

You children/masses have suffered from the demonic deception and have allowed the low fallen stars to dictate unto you what is now their truth, which makes no sense, in movies. In these movies, they are telling you where they are leading you to, as they want you to spiritually/mentally accept this way which enslaves you on every level.

You must wake up as those who are asleep will not be spared if they are caught un awake. The blood savages of Rome have come out into the open with their darkness, displaying many of these things in their entertainments. Their churches, their organizations, gangs and, the serpent/government are all one in organization.

The symbols(signs) are all affiliated, if you look at them clearly when reading the world that you are living in, with spiritual-mental mind of common sense.

Christ's mass shall be in this day when the Lord descends to give his stars his light-enlightenment. This is a blessed day, and time for all on earth to finally see the Sun. As the wicked have done all that they were allowed to do, to eclipse M3 from showing, thy flaming face.

It is the Lord only, who carries the torch of lighting-enlightenment. He is the bearer of the spirit-mental in great men, who are destined to win. The mass deception has poured unto generations of those who have turned away from what they once knew to be TRU. They have backslid into the darkness of being as everyone else, who believes in nothing/darkness.

They have lost all spiritual-mental substance, and have been set back away from the daylight. He has been made to believe that he has been evolving into a better life. However, he has been spiritually-mentally lowered into a slum, the same places that many of the poor are much too used to living in.

You have accepted the foolishness which diminishes your ability to grow. Surely, as wheat looks like the weeds, you shall use discernment to determine by the way, which are rightful wheat or wrongful weeds.

Who can make any mistake, that has the Lords good mind-3ye to see?

Everywhere that the wise shall turn there will be an evil person looking to deceive them with lies. They will seek your sympathy so that you empathize and they can cheat you a second time. You must become wise to the same old lies that have been being told if you want to become free of the covering darkness-deception.

It is a sweeping plague of wickedness, and you will see this infection of senseless, hatred in many disabled minds-souls, bodies-masses of men. Many of them will even try to pretend to be different, with the demon hidden deep within their intentions.

You must be able to sort them out when fishing for realness. Know that time/the Lord shall reveal all things that you must become aware of, which shall keep you spiritually-mentally moving ahead of the foolish.

Let them pick their poison as it shall be the same deadly poison that they have gotten onto their own hands, and into their own 3yes-minds. As the Lord has a fix, for all foolish broken things.

These men who claim to be wise have been leading your minds-3yes downward, up until now.

Where, are the shining inner-lightened-enlightened stars/jewels/kings to thy assembled bodies-masses?

The wicked follow M3, as they know who I AM and, want to take from M3, what I have come to give thy children spiritually-mentally. Ye shall hand them thy spiritual ladder and watch from above, while they ascend unto M3.

I tell you lightened ones, to not go down the dark path, to give the wicked in darkness-ignorance light. You may lose your own spirit sight-light when you have traveled too deep into their darkness-ignorance behind them.

This is the pure reason that there is the 7th day-star of prophecy, as none shall go into hell or come out without M3. I AM the key, and word which giveth men spiritual-mental enlightening elevation.

I tell you that those who are deceived in this day are those who turn from the enlightenment/light which has cometh 4th to shine, and polish 4ths/kings/jewels.

The once believers have become the non-believers. Those who have long loved others have become filled with hatred just as everyone else. Where do you find strength in being, and doing what all others are doing, even if it is failing you tremendously?

Satan is more than easy to find, simply look at the ways of the people who are in a hurry to be your equal company.

Evil is prevalent in ignorant/dark people. They roll in it like pigs in mud, making sure that they are covered from head to toe, in every inch of vile darkness/ignorance. There is nothing on their times-minds schedule, other than which is the best way to blind those of you, who are able to see them.

The wicked do not like to be seen because those wise minds-3yes that can see them flee from them al while exposing them to light. The sensible wise of truth want nothing to do with the wicked of deception-darkness.

How can you be considered to be a wise man by other wise men, if you spend time with idiots? These different classes are not held in mind by the host, at the same exact time. One must be active, for the other to be sent out. If there is light, then the darkness will depart.

Steadfast and strong are the bodies/masses/churches of Christ as they are a sturdy frame of mindful stars/jewels/kings, which cover the Universe with their lighting likeness.

The solar lights of the mind-soul have been found by new Atom/Atomic light, which blasts off into flight. Those lights which began to shine within thy hexagon hemisphere shall come up, one star at a time.

Children, do not allow those who have their wicked hands in thy masses/bodies/churches to manipulate and fool you with their deceiving words, and teachings of M3.

They will tell you that I AM not TRU. However, this is for you to become enlightened and decide within your own mind-3ye. They will say that they are M3 spiritually-mentally, without having the wisdom to tell you, children, these vital things which will save you from suffering and pain.

Do they really know, or do they pretend to know and follow thy prophecy, as it is revealed? Do the wicked not take full control of what thy dark-ignorant, masses-bodies-churches do not know?

Do not look too deep into the archaeology of the Annunaki-Angels. This is a parallel story of the TRU A NEW/ANU who fights against the evils/darkness/ignorance of the systematic giants, which have taken a stronghold of mankind's masses-bodies-churches. These Nephilim have wrapped their massive hands/servants all around thy bodies of low mind/souls/lights.

It is now time for the lights to break free of the deceiving lies, which have been training them to be the dead masses-bodies and tombs of the dark-ignorance.

Hallowed and hated, is he who has not been caught in the dark wave of deceptiveness. Along with the other dumb drowning demons, which will soon be all washed up. For this is no competition, even as the wicked can look over to see that the wise are winning.

Ye are not angry with them; neither envious. As we know that they are fools without purpose. They will not spiritually-mentally come up with much of anything which puts themselves to good use, any time soon.

He who loves himself will want to see the truth. As true love is being awakened, and standing upright ready to march with light.

You will need light so that you do not lead a march in darkness to stumble on a rough, jagged stone of deception.

As there are many trapping snares, slow snails, and low snakes on ground level waiting for ye to fall.

Let us hold Christ's lighting-enlightening mass. As you shall come together to shed light onto thy darkened church's/masses/lights. For thy church is as thy woman, and it is thy body which gives birth to stars.

Do not winners have a job, just as losers. The enlightened are still known as the winners, as the evil hater is known as the ignorant loser?

Behind every successful, strong Lion-king, there is the following pack of weak hating hyenas biting at his ankles with their broken teeth. However, ye will manage to shake them off to keep moving forward toward the finish line. Where the kings/4th who have already crossed over, are waiting for him in the new the Jerusalem.

Surely, there is much risk in this race for glory. There are obstacles, and snares which have snatched and trapped many men along the way, that were traveling the road behind M3.

Deception is a spiritual-mental decision, as ye who makes the right decision is not deceived by any false tongue or image. He has been raised up, by the father of mankind into spiritual-mental moral righteousness.

He sees what is transpiring, and has spiritually-mentally separated himself away from the dark-ignorant masses. He knows whose hand has raised him up from the dead into a life of peace, love, and giving.

He has seen his father do, conquer and accomplish many things on his own. He sees that the spirit-mental within H.I.M./The Fathering Universe is also with, and in him through trans mutated DNA, and transfigured intellectual-wisdom.

Many of you children have accepted this dark deception out of your fears, and ignorance in pleasing your enemy. You have stepped into the darkness, with the insecure fear of how you will be viewed by others, for holding the light of truth.

You have chosen to be ignorant as everyone else, fearing that the dark forces which rule the world would persecute you. You have been brainwashed, with movies of the sweeping Mob.

The wicked have used your dreams to deceive you into a deep sleep so that you will see their nightmare. Now, you will not awake, to the loud sound of spirit-mental guidance.

The 7th trumpet has sounded, and the veil has been relieved from the 3yes-minds of the deceived blind men who have become mice, and the new word has come with the new day-star of light. This light shall ignite Christ's Masses of Lights, which are the masculine minded, enlightened masses/bodies/stars of Christ (The Lord).

Let the bodies/churches/masses of Christ raise up into 1 colossal figure. The Church shall stand, and many hallowed-enlightened, men with mentals/spirits shall come together with M3. You stars are thy legs/pillars of fire, and thy Hebrew are holy bronze feet. Why do you children allow the wicked to raise the blonde woman up above M3, the Lord?

Where there is to be an outer Hebrew man who has become the Lords in-lightened jewel/king. There will be a blonde Viking, that the wicked will look to pair thy spiritual-mentally gifted men with. They are known to be from the very bottom, as the mothering 0's/Nuns of Rome.

Why do you think that you see rich slave Hebrew men paired with them? As this is not his own decision, but instead a life decision made by those who own him.

These women of Rome only come to thy men-kings for their gold data, through their celestial DNA. They want to take the Lord's jewels/kings back home to Rome. It is when you become spiritual-mental kings/4th that you will see many of these underhanded things unfold before the mind-3ye. You shall explore hell no more, because of what he has promised, with and in the future/father.

He is hated by many ignorant-dark men who don't even know him for possessing this blessing of spiritual-mental wealth which is able to take a man on wings to where he needs and wants to be. I tell you that the Lords will shall coincide with what's in a man's mind/3ye, giving him all that he needs. For in his will is wealth in all worlds, which shall be open for you children to climb into.

The demons of deception are in every corner lurking to take over the life of another with their immoral wickedness. They are forceful, which is why you must be active at spiritual-mental will. They will try to make you think that you children don't fit in, because they are all into the same drowning, deceiving darkness.

However, it is they who live in darkness/ignorance that do not fit into the class of enlightened stars. This gives an answer to the reason that they have followed the low way, looking for a higher way, which was said to be a different road.

They did not know that there were many deceiving wicked things lurking in the darkness, waiting with a lure to reel them in, within their time of suffering. These dark creatures of the abyss were watching all along to see what you possessed and what you do to manage yourself. They want to know your source, and who blesses you because you do not go through any of the wicked, to gain good favor.

It is those enlightened stars-men who are in covenant with the Lord that the wicked come from the mountains to employ.

Just as they had done under the Sun during the time of thy 4th/King Solomon. Do you not remember?

The blood beast will come for thy lighting jewels-stars and come again. However, M1cha3L shall come for you with, and in time/the Lord. For this day is mandated, as the sun is mandated to shine.

If you look into the sky around you, then you shall see the churches, and bodies of jewels-stars within each, and every one of you children waiting to be exposed to light-enlightenment.

I have told you, children, that thy angels/angles/spirits are here with M3, and you are 1 with them. You are the Lord's children and are 1 within H.I.M-M3.

Where is the competitive hand that stands against, he who serves the Lord?

In days to come, when history is said and done. You shall have none, that will have done anything comparing to the wonderful, compelling works of his composing hands.

I tell you, to know the spirits that you are talking to, by what they are proposing unto you to take from them. As a high, or low spirit-mental will almost certainly offer-suggest something appealing to a mortal mind/body/soul.

Do not be fooled by those who want to be close to you. What will the wise do with the comfort of a fool? Why would a fool who wants to continue being so, want to speak in the company of wise men?

I will tell you, people, that there could be no other reason for this than to speak nonsense among wise men, and/or to entice them with what had enticed, and tempted him along the way.

Can you see not, the downward cycling of an idle mind that's running on Empty?

It makes decisions with its life, based on what material bribes that it has received from another. It has no characteristic moral value invested into anything, of substantial mentality-spirituality.

You children are the dark churches-bodies. As those descending, enlightening stars-spirits, in which you shall allow to manifest are of the 1's in 10. They are thy descending spirits/mentals of the ancestral-eldering men, which now must raise up to ascend.

You must ready your minds-3yes to take spirit-mental flight into the sunlight. Where all things about you, and your history become able to see in the future.

The present life that you live and the father-future are revealed to you. The future/Lord holds the key to all 3 of these metaphysically relative things, which are obtainable through purification, and meditation.

A real man shall exercise his spiritual-mental right to pick his road, as his choice shall lead to more decisions that he will have to make within the future. Nevertheless, he will exercise this right wisely, because he is real spiritually-mentally.

He shall leave a message behind for you children to spiritually-mentally possess. It is the bread that the Lord has given him to give unto you, and you shall regurgitate this word of truth that shall feed, and nourish the many dark minds/souls.

Do not be deceived by the flashing light, and sparkle from man-made jewels. Instead, become enlightened by the flashing enlightenment of wisdom that comes shining from the jewels/kings/4th.

Children of discipline, do nothing for those nations which will do nothing to raise you up. Do not clock into work for them, as they are not the real knights watch.

The real watchers are the hands of time who have come for he who sees, believes, and receives thy word from them and has clocked in as a watching hand with the Lord forever.

When will you children become spiritually-mentally solid-real, to have enough of your minds-3yes being manipulated, and twisted by the enemies implanted wickedness? Let go, of your minds-souls curses of deception to receive your spiritual-mental blessing. It is the only way out of the darkness-ignorance that you are stuck below in.

He who does not work does not eat, as this is true. However, this does not mean to go out and eat from any and every hand that wants to feed you. He who eats forever has a mind full of lighting wisdom.

There is a difference between having a job and working for the Lord. One is work that you will have forever, and the other is toil through a government-serpent temp agency.

One will be a part of history. However, the other shall be forgotten the moment that they leave, and cannot return to the office building. One works from the spiritual-mental, mind-3ye of time, as the other is given a scheduled directive, and told to show up on time.

Do you not know the difference between having a job, and having a purpose?

One shall outlast the other, as the wise men shall outlast the ignorant. The deception of thy masses is the dark spiritual-mental deception of the nation's kings/jewels.

Men who would have otherwise become enlightened-lights of thy churches-bodies, if somehow, he would have not allowed the corrupt serpent-government into his mind.

You now know these things because you have been given enlightening-light. As I were once upon time trapped in darkness. However, I climbed out, into the Levitical-Levitating spirit-mental of star-sunlight, to become the 1 Fiery Metaphysical Jewel/King/3ye/Mind above, which sees, and has seen it all.

The Heads & The Hands

The heads and hands are the mentals/spirits, and servants of the Lord's church. Their minds-3yes have not been manipulated and, pulled away into wickedness. These are the lord's kings, and workers who perform from gold thoughts, deeds of fine good. They are the able meek servant-hands of the Lord who are fit to uplift and lead on.

Whatever dwells in the mind of a man shall come out in his works of the heart. For if his mind is weak, then his heart will be more vulnerable. He will not move forward, to engage anything of greatness. He will talk the talk. However, he will not walk the spiritual-mental walk. This separates the Lords inner lightened kings, from he who is dark with ignorant matter inside. Sealed are those whose minds have spiritual direction unto thy kingdom, as they are spiritually-mentally sealed with the plan of the Lord, and shall act on these inspirations in fine, exceptional deeds.

The wise can see by what a man does, what's on his mind-time. Whatever harbors is in a man's head shall reflect in his hands, as these are his TRU intentions pouring out within his planned agenda. What do you do daily with your mind-time, and hands?

Who do you use your minds educated thoughts for? If you do not use these things for the Lord, then you have lost your way to the new day-star. You have lost balance and fallen below into a dark pit, to be left behind, alone and gone astray.

He who opens his mind-3ye also has opened his hand for the Lord's gift, and promise as he lives it to its fullest.

The Lord has many retrieving hands as they are also his watching minds-3yes that are ready, and waiting for his spiritual-mental instruction. If the head is in the wrong place, so will the hands be. For thy heads/leaders, and hands/hooks are 1, as a priest is a spiritual head, and a hand is a servant king.

Who else is the servant king, who will serve those who have served M3?

The hands and minds of time are with spirit as this is what levitates them into the land of kings. Where their minds/hands receive the gift of immortality. He who serves time-the Lord and not the earthly serpent-government in his minds-hands deeds has repented.

The wicked are with the agenda of the serpent/government in their minds-hands. Just as the righteous are with the plan of the Lord, in their minds-hands. All are sealed by their minds/hands works, and the spiritual-mental servants/kings know who they are, and where to find themselves.

The dirty minds/hands do the ignorance that they do so that you real men will fall into becoming like them. Therefore, if you do fall, the wicked will no longer have to worry about you coming for what is yours.

Surely, it is within this lightened day, that you shall be able to see the heads-hands of ignorance clearly. It is the fool who has wasted his mind-time, pretending as though he is doing something of relevance. The fact that you righteous minds/hands stay busy working in truth, on your grind to become enlightened jewels/kings, seems to bother with his dark mind. Children, continually remind your minds, not to do what the minds of fools do.

Do not become consumed with them, as their minds-3yes are consumed with vile thoughts of you men. The wicked are in anger because they cannot reward themselves with your failure. You strong, spiritual-mental minds-hands have pulled through while completing all that you had to do, for the Lord-Universe.

For your reward is timeless, and ions/A eons more than the salt that the spineless snail, shall receive from M3.

As the wise who have opened their minds-3yes for thy spirit-mental have opened their hands, and hearts to receive what is solid, and TRU.

The mind is with the soul, as thy flesh servant hands-kings are with the bodies-stars. The priestly spirit-mental is present with the mind-soul, while the harping hearts fleshly vocal way of expression is given through clean hands/servant kings. You will see many men with seals on their heads, and hands of the outer flesh, so do not look for a mark to be there.

For this is a spiritual-mental war, and the seal of the head and hand is of the inner mind, and its exterior lighting works. As one will always be accompanied by the other. Therefore, it shall be difficult to be fooled by what any man tells you, from the words of his own mouth. When ye already see what the word of the Lord says, in its TRU meaning.

The heads/minds/3yes, and hands are of the celestial bodies-churches. Those who see thy word are committed to the honor and, the glory of their Lord-Father, as they know where I AM. He has the insightful mind of a marching Martian. He is a confined lecturing lectual, with the metaphysical mind of superior Intel.

The scrambling of thy word and thy numbers-stars is evident. The two three-23 is M3, the Father-33/6. The three sixes-666 is M3, the 36(The 3ye-Sun, and bodies-stars of the Father-Universe-6).

What do you children have on minds/heads, hearts, and hands? Is it blood or life?

What have you submitted yourselves unto, because you felt that it was paying you more attention, and money at that time?

Admittedly, I know what many of you have submitted yourselves unto. The serpent/government has tried to force M3 into the submission of these sinful acts so that I would be unable to come unto you.

This is the wicked game that is being played to keep your souls/minds in darkness. However, I have seen their snares, that they have planted for M3 to fall into.

The serpent/government has done a decent job, in making all of these incidental wicked acts that it does look to be coincidental. However, this is only in the casting blindness of a fool, the enlightened see what is calculated, and TRU

Any wise man can see that the serpent/government implants wicked heads with dark minds, and servants with sinister hands to do planned wickedness against the ignorant, innocent. Leaving worlds of devastated people in fear, wondering where the root of these wicked acts of terror stems from.

However, the righteous heads with the enlightened mentals are the servants with blessed hands and prophetical wise insight. These men are able to see where the hands/servants of the perpetrator are roaming about.

I tell you, children, to clean your heads, and hands of blood and nonsense. For the kingdom of the Lord is near, and hear. Keep an open, focused mind-3ye on M3, and remove your hands away from sinister acts. You shall then be brought up with the Lord-6, by the head, and grasp of his hallowed enlightening spirit-mental.

Those kingly men with the spirits-mentals of the high priests shall speak the word of a living king, unto upcoming living kings.

He who has then transfigured into a spirit-mental king/jewel/4th, shall take this word from his head-mind into his deeds-hands, and give it unto the others, so that they may also become free, wise Priestly-heads, and Kingly servant-hands.

Precious
Mentals/Metals

Gold is the new age of magnesium lighting intellect, for it is the head of thy church-house of Israel. As bronze clay is the bottom of thy feet/ground and the old age for those children who have been again taken into bondage-Egypt. He who has thy mutable spirit is gold as he shall walk through fire on the water in burnt flesh. He knows the old word, as he shall know thy new and, TRU word.

I tell you that the future-father shall only speak of himself, the future-father. He shall not dwell on the old(past), or new-present testament, as the revealing is all that is TRU, in its future Testament. The son of man did not quote from the Bible. However, instead, he did quote directly from the father-Universe, and he was criticized and crucified for thy word not appealing to the deaf ears of ignorant men.

Did not thy Sun-son come forward with thy word to those blaspheming men which told him, that he was walking in blasphemous sin, because they could not metaphorically comprehend the spirit-mental of M3/M1cha3l in him, back then?

The unwise men took no notice in the mind-3ye of the transfiguring spirits-mentals information, as many who claim to be spiritual-mental stars do not see.

Woe, to he who claims to be born a God as M3, the One 3rd. This is not TRU of you fallen celebrities-stars who taught these lies to blind men to satisfy your requirement for status and finances.

However, I have come to tell men. Learn, geometry to know the stars/angels-angles of the Lord by their wisdom, as their sense will be your light-enlightenment.

There is nothing that the real stars will tell you people, that will be of no good everyday common use to you. You shall know the sound of light, or dark when you hear them. The sons of confined light give life, and death with thy sword-word, they tote the word-sword as they move with the inner levitating mind-9.

Yes, he is spiritually-mentally armed, and dangerous as he has come to abduct men, women, and children. Many who choose to remain on the dark side, shall be slaughtered with thy exposing truth of scorching light which comes from thy mouth. While those who have chosen M3, shall see a life of fulfillment, and engulfing light.

He shall be chosen to live his dreams in front of the eyes of his enemies. The gift of the word shall flow through him, as fiery atoms that disburse from the lungs of a talking dragon. Ye shall purify the righteous souls-minds, and burn the wicked to dust. Allowing them to grow up anew with his truth, or die as exterminated weeds and dry fallen leaves.

The flesh of men is born no Gods as they are born into a world of darkness-sin, which is the reason that you children need to be mentally/spiritually born again. Far away from the false teachings, and evil things that you have seen were taught, and exposed to early on in life by ignorant guardians.

Let the enlightened-light kings of the age, stand in their golden intellectual mental-metal properties, with M3 in this day of rejoicing.

This day is for all men who have made a wise choice, to be spiritual-mental slaves to the serpent-government no more.

You are only able to act on what you know. Now you know. Therefore, ye must act, or be held accountable for the unaccountable. He who knows thy truth is counted, as he who knows nothing-darkness cannot be calculated with M3 among thy enlightened stars.

He who has not the wisdom of common sense has evolved back into the bronze age of bondage. Where the enemy with the agenda wants you to be slaves, beneath them. However, those men with the spirit-mental of gold have the revolving minds-heads. This is the separation of the gold, and the bronze, the wheat, and the weeds. The foundation and the lighting.

One must hold up the other so that thy house can be seen illuminating with bright light from the mountain top. Thy church is thy house, as thy house is thy church and sanctuary-body.

I AM a priest and a king. Thy house and thy church are the 1 with and in M3.

The Gold are kings of spirit-mental wisdom, as this is the age when they are raised up from among the dead masses, that are beneath the foot of the ignorant. You see, the Lords sees not your religions, he sees the masses of dark-ignorant misguided celebrating.

This gives a reason as to why the Lord condemns no nation of people, for what they do not yet know. He condemns those leaders/hands of falsehood that know his truth, who have misguided you, children. These demons are being paid to mentally breach you, sending you unknowing children back in time, into a slave age. They are spiritually-mentally, forcing you to accept the noose around your own necks before they push you.

The serpent and its dark servant-hands are propping you up on a stool for the kill.

They seek to bury all of thy gold, which they cannot possess among themselves to be as one of their own.

The word Ghost begins with a G. As the able hosts, with the Universes-Times levitating star spirit-mental belong to the Lord-God. The ghostly spirit mental of all hosted' spirits-mentals, is the 1 supreme spirit of the Lord-God.

The light of the Lord shall shine through, for you to see which are gold, and which are dark with flaws internally. You shall not fool the 3yes-Suns of the Lord-God who seeks his own golden illuminating likeness.

That which are not golden shall go at thy feet as a king's dust. Those who become golden spiritually-mentally are precious metal-mental producing, enlightened kingly jewels to M3.

A Word from the 1ˢᵗ & Last Day/Star

The last day/star has cometh, with what those who have endured have been waiting for. This is the last day that you shall be weak. This is the last day that ye shall tolerate ignorance, as this is the last day for the for ye to be of the spiritual-mental peasants. However, instead, it is the first day, for you to become spiritual-mental kings-Jewels.

This is the 1ˢᵗ day for you to rise up, as the chosen golden people that you once were, before you were spiritually-mentally broken poor of your pure culture, and origin way as jewels-kings.

However, this is the last day that you shall forget thy word. He who is wise has stopped and put down everything that he was doing, as he knows that something is coming. He has seen those stars that fly high fall down to the ground, and become of the dead.

I tell you that he who is 1ˢᵗ and last is who you shall see within the minds-3yes sight. This is the arriving day/star to be glad about, as this is the day/star of promise. He has the revealing word that you would have to be a spiritual-mental fool not to see, to identify that he is the 1 and 2 in M3.

The water-father, the fire- sun and, the spirit airs are the elements with, and in earth kings/4ths-men. The 7th day/star of revelation is the stand of the anointed 1, as he has had enough! He has again, as the flesh son of man. Externalized biblical prophecy, with none other than the meek stars/hands/servant-kings of the time/Lord.

Again, it has been written, as it has been done, by the 1/Lord/7 Days-Suns/Universe.

The Lord

Is

Greatness

Certainly, you have heard many times of how great the Lord is; however, he is even greater than many men can come to imagine. He is beyond great, as ye is the word which the words of great men cannot yet explain.

He is the shower of fiery hot stars, and rains cold waters. He brings down giants so that they shall never stand again, as he is the truth of light, and the air-spirit in the breath of life.

He is Adam/Man/Heaven and Eve/Woman/Earth, as ye is Atom/light and Evening/darkness. He was the demonstration and definition in Job's testament of what a man on his job is. He is the natural element which is with the sequential mental-spirit in men, as there is no higher hand than his to lift the fallen. Men who have walked with him in a fiery mind have seen their destiny unfold before their eyes.

Greatness is he, as it is revealed with Time. He is the greatness in all of mankind, for it is with the 3ye of the Lord that kings are able to teach these mystical things unto you. For there is only one priestly king of the Universe.

However, the earth has many priestly kings/jewels, which shall soon be discovered by a deserving hand.

Surely, ye is marvelous as the wise minds shall marvel on his majesty's majestic wisdom and insight.

There is no brighter light for any to depend upon.

Search for the lord in the silence of confinement and ye shall find him confined within the righteous seeing mind-3ye, trying to get you to listen to H.I.M.

He is wise and therefore, e sends signs/stars before the minds/3yes of those men with the common sense to see them shining. He who lifts his head away from the worlds shining material jewels of gold, and diamonds.

All who are great become great by the hands of the lord, as he who is great knows that the Lord is even greater than he. This is how he has come thus far on his path without falling, and not getting up again.

He has paid mindful attention that hard works alone does not achieve the TRU blessings of successes greatness. However, it is the charismatic, aristocratic, characteristic elemental of the Lord, which leads the way into the land of milk and honey.

Have not the 3yes/minds of wise men marveled on the Lord's greatness in nature? There is no greater mind/3ye in a man than that which is in a man that reflects on him in greatness. For great minds think alike, as he who thinks like the Lord.

Children, I tell you that if you want greatness. You must then consult with he who specializes in giving men glory. Focus not on natural, literal imperfections, for ye may not receive the overall message.

It is the Lord who can take he who is imperfect, and mold him as potters clay into a complete image of lasting perfection. Where has ye not taken men from, and made them into kings?

Truly, I say that the Lord does these works using his hands with regularity, as he has given a blessed life to he who has struggled regularly without complaint, or conscious sin.

The Lord comes to gather what is right, to make it great.

I say, let's make the Lord in heaven great on earth again, as he shall break barriers to give you a new way that you have never seen before.

No man shall find this place of greatness, without the spiritual-mental light of the lord. I cannot speak for the false gods of other men. However, the Lord-God, Is Ra El of he who Is real is indeed great all the time.

He is the only lord to the real, but never to the false. He wears not false jews or gold on his body. His body is his church, and all which comes in, and goes out must be pure with golden spiritual/mental intent.

Greatness has been misidentified and mis defined among spiritually/mentally poor men who have come from nothing-darkness. The mind which comes from nothingness will continue to think of all to be this way if it does not pay him in his low nations dividing dividends.

TRU greatness is in history. It is to have your name written in the Book of Life, as the Lord writes his never-ending story of kings. Riches have defined many weak men, who were weaker without them. Now that they have riches you better not say anything to this spoiled coward, who has never had any power.

I tell you that a great father will fight so that his children are able to see him. However, if they cannot manage to see him right away, because of the many distractions, he will leave his word so that they shall remember H.I.M. forever.

There is nothing which angers him more than those who take the remnants of his church/body away from him. As these are the children of Israel/The Lord, who shall blossom in his stead of greatness. He who has been through dark, tough times is humbly grateful, as he reflects from where he is today. He has trotted a long way with sweat dripping, and blistering feet.

He has seen hell, which has brought him to the Lord's door for help. Mortal men have repeatedly failed him with their 3yes/minds of sin.

They have led and let him down, but he has gotten right up and did not continue to fall into nonsense with them.

For in this kind of sheer will and determination, there is nothing more than the Lord's greatness to revere. It is what has kept thy men/kings planted here on earth as strong trees.

The greatness of the Lord brings tears of pain and joy. Blessed with greatness is the slave in spiritual/mental deliverance, who is given a gift to give to the world.

What is without the Lord? For he is all. Is he not?

TRU greatness is in the 3ye-mind of the beholding Marathon runner with spirit/mental torch, that knows his influential potential. As he who has lost his mind has lost the battle between light and darkness.

Greatness is measured with a scale that weighs men's deeds. The leveled scale which balances out humanity, through the inner galactic characteristic principal, and spiritual/mental morality.

The are many recorded stories of the Lord's greatness, as he has reigned through righteous men and their next of kindred. Generation after generation, and season among season.

He has given hopeless men new reason and has scattered the minds/3yes of wicked men. Sending them out of his sight wandering in many directions, searching for water to quench their agonizing thirst.

I tell you that the burning shall become worse than any hellfire for the fool who does not pay tribute to the Lord, by recognizing his spiritual-mental hosts.

For he has ignored thy messengers; therefore, he has not received thy message and word of liberal liberation. He does not recognize the presence of the Lord in the flesh. As he does not acknowledge, accept, and recognize in his mind/3ye and, heart that the Lord is the greatest of them all.

I tell you, children, not to worship thy flesh host. Instead, work in the Lord's name, if you seek TRU prosperity. There is no greater prosper, than the prospering blessing that ye gives unto another. I say to you that if you are greater and more significant than the Universe.

Then allow M3 to see you materialize into gold, your thoughts without M3 in your mind/3ye guiding you with thy spiritual/mental enlightenment/light. Nothing is what ye shall find in his view as nothing- darkness will be in the mind/3ye of the man who departs from M3, the enlightened 1.

Which star is able to give off more enlightenment/light, than the ever-burning Sun above in the spiritual/mental sky, and below in the earthly mind/3ye?

Many men who have come up before you enrolling children have blended their chemical compounds into testament, which leads to greatness/the Lord. History/His story does not lie, as many accounts have been given by the numbers/stars who stand in faith, and truth while holding his word.

None can say that they receive the word of the Lord, who reject to take it from thy host who brings it 4[th.] How can ye take thy water, without the cup that he has given to drink of it?

Allow greatness to be a discovery within yourselves where you find and unlock its priceless, valuable contents. As a wise man has seen folly/foolishness, but a fool has not yet been wise. However, what great men define as knowledgeable, great, Love, or truth. Have all been redefined in the minds-3yes of the masses by those wicked rulers, who chase behind in the dust of greatness/the lord.

This is the coward mind of demons who are hard pressed and possessed on being what they are not. These are the wicked ordinary, average men who hate when they see the illumination of greatness within extraordinary real men.

These demons will do anything unnecessary to take this glow of greatness away from him. They will send their wicked women to snare him. They will send out spies with lies to discredit his masses-bodies of works and elevating movement.

I tell you that any man who sees not the greatness in the Lord sees not the greatness or importance in himself. He is blind to all spiritual and natural wealth.

Does not the lord awaken the minds-3yes of wise men, for a new day of meditating contemplation?

Great is the limitless mind-3ye, which sees nothing in its sight that will keep it from levitating, glowing, and growing. Do you children know that you are the superstars that are to save the world from darkness?

It is in you, to learn that you are the greatest of all people as you are the lights to thy church-body, and this is the greatest show on earth.

For those of you who are laying in the bottoms of hell because you are in a cell of some sort. If you know where thy light is, you can still shine, and be found from where you are. Sunlight shines into the smallest dark places if it is allowed in to do its works of spiritual worth. Great is the determination of the jewel/king who has been dropped into the mud, and digs his way out to see his own shining reflection.

Is this not a story of great perseverance and spiritual/mental preservation? This is a TRU soldiers' story of destined greatness and glory.

For, he has come to be flanked by a worshiping garment of stars/jewels/kings. They shall align around him, as lamps of giving enlightenment/light. They shall provide him their hand, and resourcefulness in the name of the Lord who multiplies.

The grateful are the great and gifted. As they reflect on the many great things that Lord has brought them through and done for them. Ye savors and reminisces on the moments of his nonexistence as he remembers the first, and last day of his prison sentence.

This was in the day that the Lord had come unto him and said, "Come work for M3, I have a greater opportunity for you to see, and be seen." "Surely, when thy lift you. You shall see, and all eyes shall see you also. For what is held up high into thy sky's light, is seen by all minds-3yes with common sight."

This is the greatness of the above and below. There is no hell, it is only your fiery in conviction solar mind/soul which shall roam until it is consumed. If it stays low/slow, you shall die a second time. This has not been changed by those hands that are without the key to death, and immortality. He who is lifted in the Lord's name receives more than fame and money.

He has stood up for something different, other than that in which everyone else was going, and following within ignorance-darkness.

He is much too enlightened, and on his way unto greatness to take a fall. He is on his way to the Lord, who is indeed the Greatest.

Great is his name, and the many spiritual-mental names-men in which he has sent, as his hands to do his works of testimonial greatness. He has carried his own kingly cup to the Lord's table filled to the overflowing brim, with the blessings of water/wisdom.

How can you define what you cannot identify?

First, you must know what you are seeing, before ye can begin receiving from its enlightenment, to go gospel unto others its TRU meaning. A king who kneels not to a priest strikes himself with his own sword.

A younger brother who submits not to the given way of the elder who has the priestly way of the father/Lord has disowned and has become disowned by his own royal family-spirit & blood.

Do not allow the wicked to deceive you of your greatness by giving you their lies. All while, they pretend to live your moral spirit truth. You are at the bottom, even though you descend from the top. They are at the top of the world but are on the very bottom spiritually and morally. They've come from material riches which are worthless, but you come from nothing/darkness with a priceless spirit.

You are the children of greatness/the Lord as the lord is great, and highly great is the lord. Let H.I.M. shine through you as a Father/Universe of outer darkness shines through his suns/stars/sons of enlightening-light.

Allow his light of greatness come out in your spiritual fight against the forces of darkness/ignorance. If I tell you, that the Lords following stars/kings are leads, then this means that he who follows M3 is a leading king/4th-truth. There is no other place for any man to find this kind of greatness, as the real shall walk out of hell with M3, guiding them with enlightenment spiritually-mentally.

How can America-Babylon be a great place while you, the slaves are not doing so great?

Do not the people first need to be great for their place of living to be clean?

TRU's greatness is measured by the scaling minds-3yes of metaphysical kings/hands. This is the greatness of the mind, which brings life. This is the great mind of a man who lives because he lives with truth as he has suffered and bled to get from where he was at, to where he has cometh.

He has not found a reason to curse the Lord when things are not going right for him. He knows that life is short but not short enough to not have any reasonable substance added to it by its developer. He has studied the works of the creating developer and has seen it be comely.

Great is he who holds time/the lord in his mind, as he is spiritually-mentally aware to not lose, or abuse it as it is present. Children, the wicked of the earth-mother will try to erase the legacy and word of your father by, renaming you and not giving you the right spiritual-mental pictures of him.

However, it is up to you children to keep his spirit-mental enlightenment lit in your minds-3yes. As the dirty wicked hands of the mother/earthly seed seek to dispose of all his memorable remaining remnants, which have the fathers reminding reflection.

Everyone is a hateful slave in this day, they all do the same wicked things.

However, if you do not happen to see them, then they will say that they are different from the rest of the hateful wicked. Watch as they will do wickedness at every chance that they can if they do not think that anyone has a 3ye on their secrecy.

You have to watch carefully because they are the passive aggressive sinners who lie, that are out looking to bring down the real men of greatness who tolerate their weakness. The wicked are watching the TRU stars to see in which way that they are going so that they can jump in front of them hoping to win.

However, the hands of greatness/the Lord move fast, as they waste no time attacking the enemy, with thy completed works of and proofs of math-fact.

Let the wicked fester in their dark anger, and idolatry. The Lord sees them not, as they are stuck with internal minds-souls of ignorance-darkness.

I tell you that the wise fear nothing as they have the knowledge of its discovery, and root existence. He can smile at the enemy, knowing that he is the TRU Great king/Jewel, which they claim to be. He knows that they can see the lighting wisdom that he brings 4th to the table, for all to be able to see as they eat, and drink of its grateful, goodness, and purity.

The Lord has done many great things for you children, and ye will see them in the raw spectacle if you look at life clearly. As most men who have walked through hell, cannot begin to tell you of what they have been through without shedding a tear. As the reflection is so close and dear to his expressive heart/art. It has molded and built him level by level, levitating his mind to spiritually-mentally think in the way of greatness/the lord.

Children of IsRa El, the worlds wicked people, can see greatness within you, and they want to stop it if possible. It is a light of anointing that people are able to see, to know when the lord is blessing a man with the wisdom of prosperity. They can see thy light in his face shining, and as prophecy unfolds this inner light/enlightenment becomes much brighter, until it can no longer be contained, and must be let out to shine in truth.

There are wicked, ignorant/dark people who have a fear of what is to be naturally. Therefore, they go around the world spiritually-mentally reprogramming everyone and everything, to make the world walk into their wicked, ignorant/dark way.

There is no greatness in ignorance. What will a fool use from his mind, to become great?

These words are from he who giveth them light, as he is the word of enlightenment that makes sense to wise minds-3yes. The Sun/son has already come to speak of the past, which was in the present. Now, the father/future of Time himself has cometh, of which Yeshua had spoken.

The Revelation is now. As it is now at its last day, however before there can be a resurrection of the pure, there must be revealing of truth.

How will you know, who will be resurrecting you?

From which dead, does he speak of raising to life? You see, you must know these things before the Lord can resurrect you spiritually-mentally from among the dead/ignorant. Indeed, he is great if you know where to seek him.

However, do not go to the graveyard to sit in wait for the flesh of the dead to rise, as you will be wasting the given time-mind that you must use to search for TRU greatness/the lord/M3.

Do you not know that men wrote the Bible? It is a book, while thy word is in history with the Lord. ALL books have literal flaws that your eye can see, as it was edited by the hands of English men but the hands-servant kings of the Lord had written it. Even so, there are minor flaws in many things that are otherwise perfect. Even within you jewels/kings, as what has not minor flaw may be artificial/cloned.

What do TRU's visionary artist see that you people do not?

Kings/Jewels have a spiritual-mental reflection to see an opportunity that allows you to see perfection, within imperfection using the vision of artistic wisdom in connection. You will see fulfilling perfection, where a creative artistic perfectionist is never satisfied with his own creation of greatness.

This is the envisioning mind-3ye of a genius, who sees what the future needs for him to do. Even though during the time of its creative production, to many unleveled minds, it was not yet officially a well-known, household commodity.

However, only to a select chosen few who were blessed, and unbiased enough to view a TRU masterpiece.

Give praise to he who naturally cures what needs healing, and gives instruction to what needs discipline. Spiritual-mental transfiguration comes in shining-enlightening transcendence to wise men, who are on the road destined to greatness/the lord.

This road has been again paved for them with thy TRU word of revealing gold. He shall m33t M3 at the crossroad where there are multiple metaphysical kings/men/jewels, linking with other real characteristically flawless spiritual/mental kings/men/jewels.

Men of greatness focus not on the past or current events. He focuses instead on the future/father, as he has to keep moving forward without stagnation.

The past has nothing left for him, and the present has been exchanged for lies, which have tricked many minds-3yes out of seeing their future/father of greatness.

The future/father tells what is great in history, as greatness can only be measured by time/the lord. It is only he, the Lord who defines it, that shall give it to men because it is his own to continue to own. M3/M1cha3l is the sword/word blade of the holy trinity, as ye is the spirit-mental of the begotten sun/son/1.

Thy sun of God in the sons of man is the light in the darkness, the immortality in mortality, life in death. The spirit within the carnal, an enlightened/lightened jewel/king, within the flesh.

What is not of greatness/the lord, within this kind of levitating spiritual transfiguration?

Great is the unbroken law, and order of the numbers/stars and nature. Great is the unbroken prophecy, and thy kings/hands that bring it 4th.

Greatness is an understatement for the works of the lord. He is the word because there are no words to describe the magnitude of H.I.M. Colossal, the juggernaut is what some see the great 1 to be, however, he is extremely greater in mass as he continues growing massively at a vast rate.

Children, always try to look on the bright side, to see more than what meets the minds/3yes of the many blind, who seek to be great in their own way.

This is where they have lost and forsaken themselves, as their own crooked way is the way of ignorance-darkness. Greatness has a straight forward steadfast approach, all while maneuvering obstacles on a windy, winding dark road. Greatness becomes better and new, as ye ages with time like ripened wine.

The Lord has designed, and created all things, even though he has subcontracted you, royal loyal men, to do some of his masonry/missionary work for him.

However, his objective is to clear out the old to renovate and renew you with stronger, better spiritual/mental lighting material.

There are no breaks on this journey unless you become broken and are spiritually-mentally unable to continue on because you have lost your senses. This is a common symptom of spiritual abandonment in those demonic souls/minds that are going below, in the opposite direction of greatness because they are chasing the worlds preoccupying foolishness.

Let us all become greater together, as we rise to the top. However, first allow us to grab hold of those rusted trotted pennies which were deemed to be worthless by those unworthy, ungrateful hands that have cast them aside, to die in the dirt.

We shall clean them off with water, and set them under the sun which will shine on them, so that they may give natural common light as the Christ mind-3ye. Love the Lord, oh, children. I tell you that he loves you, and has a lot of great gifts in store for you.

Reflect on where the hand of greatness has taken you, children, away from and has brought you unto. Get out of your social groups, that do not give you TRU enlightenment of M3.

These dark/ignorant groups are restraining your mind/3yes from going into the deep thoughts that it needs, in order to be freed from the wicked new world order of the spiritual-mental bondage/Egypt.

Why do you people look for greatness to be within your dark/ignorant cities, if there is no lighting greatness-God within you?

Greatness must be in 1 place before it is present within 2 spaces. For if greatness/the lord is in your mind-3yes, then things shall begin to change for the greater good in your cites, and lands by the hand of time/the lord. You shall come up to be kings/4ths of the 10th, to lead with the Levitical mind-9, as ye have been given thy dominion and reign of freedom to express, and voice thy word.

Allow the blessings of greatness to pour onto he who does his deeds for the Lord/greatness. As he looks to be solidified and sealed by the time-lord of the real.

Keep the lazy minds/3yes at a long arm's length. They do nothing for greatness/the lord, as they are out to destroy those men in life who aim for the stars. A fool thinks that he is working in progress for greatness. However, he is running is a circle of time/mind consuming stagnation, with a baton of shared hatred.

He shall come to realize in his mind, when he eventually sees he who is excellent passing him by, on his way to the top. He does not like the bottom, as it is too crowded with feather wearing heathens.

Birds of a feather shall flock together, as these men are the chickens which shall come home to roost. When you see chickens, then he shall know the truth, to see that he wants to be a high-flying eagle.

Children stand with M3, to be great for the Lord who is with thee. Make a final disciplined decision on how you want to live for the future/father, from this first and last day forward.

Greatness/the Lord is always available for those awakened ones, with the aligned genesis minds-3yes vision to see and achieve in abundance.

Greater is he who is spiritually-mentally able to be in you than he who is in the world.

Kingdom Cometh

The Kingdom of the Lord/Universe is at hand, as he has cometh with his Sun, and his stars. Children, it is vital that you be spiritually-mentally born into a new/Anu way of thinking if ye seek to be received into thy holy kingdom above, that which is below.

However, there is a word that you must receive in mind, to be crowned as a divine witness. Have you not heard these words before under the Sun, as they cometh from thy son of man?

Did he not warn you beforehand of the coming kingdom, of the sovereign Lord? I tell you, that the prophecy is standing before you, and shall continue long after. You who recalled up are caught up in the revealing rapture, as you have a new sight which gives your face the light of a new life.

Children, remove your heads from the cloud as you seek M3 with the wrong, evil eyes, and look for the kingdom that cometh through the cloudy fog in your minds/3yes. You have been deceived on where to find the kingdom of the lord, as he has come to relieve the sick, poor, and tired from doing what everyone else of the suffering in the head herd of ignorance/darkness is doing, with their time-mind.

Keep your minds sharpened. Therefore, they will be able to pierce the lies that the anti-Christ put in front of your eyes daily, for you to then be able minded to see who is playing the role, and wearing the robe garments of whom.

This world is another level of the school that the serpent/government uses to teach you. It is a higher school where he who passes class, shall cross over into thy kingdom.

Let, the wicked judge you, as the Lord shall judge them. Worry not of the circumstances, that you have been tempted to fall into as long as you come out of them alive.

If you believe in the coming of TRU/the Lord, then you have spiritually/mentally seen the arrival of thy kingdom on earth. Children walk not into the Luciferin temple, where there will be the lies of Satan disguised as Christianity. Lucifer wants to be M3, the Christ (Universes Crowned-Anointed) King.

What Papacy has ever possessed the kind of written wisdom that ye are now reading? There has been none, not even one. As history/his story would have recorded such prior lighting wisdom. The kingdom of the lord is not up in the sky, as that is where the high bird's dwell. It is not on the ground below, this is where slow, low serpents crawl.

In which way are you children spiritually-mentally thinking/looking?

You must become observant of your surroundings if ye are familiar with M3. The Lord needs only those men who are watchful. They are his watchers in spiritual-mental training, as nothing shall get pass them to sneak its head into thy kingdom.

There are no short cuts or slices for any of you dead, weak ends with no daylight of the 7th star-day in sight. The revealing star-day who shall show you all things, unlike those secluded churches that are shrouded in wicked mystery.

Come 4th children of the 10th as kings/4ths. The kingdom of the Lord shall cometh 4th within all of you, through spirit-mental transfiguring transformation.

I tell you, to stop and drop, whatever that it is that you are doing on the spot, and clock in with Lord/Time. As he is the 12,3,6, and the 9.

You do not want to miss this train coming into thy temple. Therefore, you should be up and ready as thy warning will be thy sounding horn and smoke. I have come to give the light that instigates the spirit/mental kingdom in you as a people.

For when it is said that thy spirit/mental is within you. It is the gift which is there waiting for you to open the door to the mind/3ye to allow it inside, to clean house and take over you. Not only beauty, but all things are in the mind/3ye of its building beholder.

It is he who allows time/the lord to build up and uplift his mind who is a TRU serving king of the Lord, within thy kingdom. You the children are thy body of Israel/The Lord, as Jerusalem is thy golden head/dome, and spirit mental sun who has thy sparkling kings/jewels/stars levitating with him.

There is no place on earth which defines M3. Israel is the Lord in thy people, and Jerusalem is M3. The first, and last of the wise jewels/stars/kings.

Where is your Messiah?

As there is no TRU Messiah, besides M3. The 1 who gave you Yeshua, as your priestly king/Messiah. It is in the pure evaluation of the character that one must liberate. He must go meditate and deliberate in devotion. It is in this time, that man must devote his mind-3ye into the direction of where he wants to eventually go.

You can only be in, whatever it is that you are able to see into. For wherever the mind/3ye/soul goes, the flesh indeed follows. If the mind is in the kingdom of the lord, then indeed the flesh is already there, or on its way.

However, if the mind/3ye/soul is in hell, then the flesh with join it there.

Come unto Jerusalem, where thy jewels/kings are steady levitating with M3, in their meditating thought. As I AM the levitating mystical, metaphysical mental thought of the father-Lord.

Let the wicked play, and act as though they are dumb to what is going on around them. However, the jewels/kings in the making can see the difference in themselves, which is incompatible to anyone else.

Do you kings/jewels not see, as I have told you how it would be in this day? Every man will resort to the same wickedness.

Do they all not tell the same lies?

Don't they all try to swerve into the lane of he who is passing them by quickly, despite what it pertains to, or where he is going? If you ask M3, of how many people have betrayed, and left M3. There will be quite a few men who shall not be allowed into thy kingdom.

The kingdom has descended close enough for you to climb unto, it is closer than it has ever been before in this 10th age. He who comes is he who returns as Priestly king of his church/house, he raises his sword/word against the wicked of Babylon for justice.

Truly, I say that a kingdom is in the dome (top of the head) of a king, as it is his wisdom which raises, and defines his kingdom spiritually-mental reality.

Do not lose your spiritual/mental reality chasing the worlds virtual lies into the dark, as ye may not be able to get back on time with thy kingly wisdom. Whatever becomes swallowed whole by a black hole, rarely ever comes back out alive.

Once it gets sucked into nonsense, it becomes of the dead men.

The spirit/mental of the lord will designate itself unto he who has discipline. You who have not this spiritual/mental discipline shall be a wanderer without thy purpose, with many unfulfilled wishes.

However, if he were walking with the lord in his spiritual kingdom, he would have plenty to offer to himself, and unto others. Because he is not with the lord, he has nothing to call his own to offer anyone.

This demon, which is blocked outside of the Lord's benevolent kingdom, only takes from the table of the lord. However, ye never gives a portion of what he has been given. This selfish man is a peasant with the inner persona of stingy wicked women who are living in scarcity. He is nothing like thy wealthy, selfless kings/jewels.

The Lord's kingdom of thy spirit kings shall reign from above, while the wicked slow/low will be beneath them. The wicked do not have the wisdom to be placed at the top of anything in the world.

However, the wicked of the Vatican puts its slow/low men into these high places, through paid education. Why do you children, who are poor of material riches, but spiritually-mentally wealthy with common sense, think that you are not at the top of the world that you live in?

This would only be coincidental to a fool who looks for excuses to problems that he is too fearful to address and refuses to fix.

This happens to be the memory loss in the mind/3yes of those losers who blasphemously call themselves men, and claim praise to the lord as though the Lord hears the words of weaklings.

There is no kingdom of God in these wicked people, for their god is in their ignorance for a dividing dollar. The freedom of wealth shall not come unto them any time soon. As they lay waste of others while chasing darkness around in a circled paragram.

Blessings to those of you who have been reading thy truth, time is on your side. There is nothing that you will not be able to do after your father has shown you the right way. You shall also come up to be great with, and in H.I.M.

His light within you will expose itself, revealing your TRU identity and TRU wealth. The Lord has given you a portion of both worlds, so that you may savor the flavor, and want more blessings from where those few tasty blessings have cometh.

Everyone is not the same, as they are not designed to be able to do the same things in life. However, you are to go in the same way of righteousness. For the Lord has a plan that comes together using multiple serving hands, which all lead to 1 purpose for the church of mankind.

Which church do you serve?

The house of Israel, or the Vatican? However, I already know your answer based on what I have seen you do unto innocent people. Therefore, whatever you say shall be held against you by the Lord/Universe of all Law.

If he has made a vow to the Lord, he must fulfill its promise that he has vowed, before ye receives what was promised unto him in inheriting blessing. Time/The Lord has mandate on all living things, in mankind as they are scheduled on his meta-levels.

For, what has not yet leveled with time/the lord displays not its amazing balancing extravagance in the mind-3ye, which spiritually-mentally stems from the Lord's kingdom.

Many of you cowardly men have done worse slander, than that of what Peter, had done to Yeshua. It was said that you must believe in what you have yet to see.

However, you did not accept the sight of M3 when you have seen thy revealing.

Surely, you shall be cast out of the mind/3ye/sun sighting of the lord/Universe and left behind in a slower/lower time-mind zone.

You shall not time-mind travel unto thy kingdom with M3. No, indeed, not for what you have not done in your deeds. You have played with the word of lord as though you did not see from his kingdom, the wicked mind-3ye manipulating in which the wicked are doing to thy children.

Israel has cometh with Jerusalem. As they are 1 head and body. Priest/King, and Church house, city, and thy lights-people. For without 1, there is no other. If the people do not follow the head of the Lord's kingdom, then they will spiritually-mentally suffer through a great tribulation, which is to come to them.

They will not have obtained the wisdom needed to go to war with the enemy. They will be knights without any sword-word, in a time of war. As a man without any spiritual-mental armor is no lighting knight-star in thy kingdom at all.

Thy kings-jewels-stars weapon of voice is a powerful blade. It is sculpted by truth fire, and by choice, he uses it with swiftness, in cutting down wickedness. It is known that men who stay focused on positivity get a lot further in life, as they do not have the slow mind/time to dwell on low thoughts.

Meditation takes time/the lord, and much practice of the practical mind in breaking the barrier of the average. There is nothing average about he who is with the kingdom of the Lord.

You are all TRU X-men. You are the extraordinary, extravagant, extracurricular. And also exiled to be kept from sharing these exceptional gifts with the world.

You are worth the Lords sacrifice as I AM worth yours. There are none in thy kingdom of kings who have not sacrificed for M3. Yes, you may think that you levitate higher than M3.

However, I AM too clever and always higher than those of you fools who believe this dark nonsense, within you to be true.

If you are high, then why can't you see thy spiritual-mental kingdom levitating beyond the mountainside, from within those dark bottom valleys, and alleyways where you are looking?

The truth is that you, as many other men, see nothing that is not physically present. You have lost your senses of manhood, which cometh with mankind. We have come through the gates of hell to get here, in order to free you from its creatures of the night in this lighting hour of enlightenment.

We are the enlightened kings-jewels of lighting wisdom. Many people will leave you good men in the dirt where they have tried to leave M3. However, I make thy arch moves to come up to the top of my game with pure light-spirit-mental speed.

Are your minds-3yes glued to M3, or your television and the many other things, distracting the 3ye-mind from thy prophecy? The Sun/son of Man is the title and the name of he who is no coward to the expressive freedom of masculine thinking. As he holds the key to the Lord's kingdom, and shall only allow spiritual-mental men to come in to eat of his wisdom.

He is the King/Men of Kings/Men, as he remains on fire, and unfrightened. No gun or weapon defines him, as thy host has come spiritually-mentally equipped with weapons of mass destruction to physically crush men.

Let, the power of the spirits/mentals/Angels, be with mortal men. As it in meditation, when a mental-angel calls on the kingdom of the lord, for the power to crush his enemies.

There is no competition for any mortal men who rise up against him.

This is the real reason that the serpent/government tries to kill, and replace the moral spirit men of the lord, with its illegitimate wicked, immoral spawned children.

Children do not become happy and go lucky while wishing nothing goes array.

Instead, be the wise as the mind-3ye of men that evaluate, and calculate their blessings with high hope that all is God. The Lord has been good to you in the past, and present for greater is he who is with the future/father.

Do you not comprehend? Have your minds/3yes climbed high enough, up thy spiritual-mental ladder for you to acknowledge-see thy presence through the knowledge that has been delivered?

Inevitably, when you have run out of time, you will do hard time. As time/the lord has bailed out on you, leaving you behind to rot in hell alone.

You have tried to bring him down, and now he wants nothing more to do with you or your low kind. He has fallen into the darkness to see the ultra-magnetic light, which exposes the transparent/phony/fake jewels.

All that peaks your interest has peeked into your mind/3yes and has stolen your attention if it of nonsense/darkness. Children of Is real, know that your Lord manifests in mental, and walks with you in this day metaphysically. His kingdom of grace has taken its place and stance on earth.

Trust in M3, when I say that even those children who speak wicked of M3, fear thy hands, and do not indeed mean what they say.

It is that many of them did not believe in anything from the beginning, and for the wicked love of money they will do, and say anything. Especially if they do not have thy spiritual-mental teachings of realness, and truth.

Why would I not continue to do something that I love to do? Those who love the Lord love the word as you also love to tell of his TRU coming kingdom.

Every good man loves when a child is loved in truth, it does not matter by whom. However, whatever is taught to a child either gives abundant life, or it destroys them.

The Lord's kingdom is life-water to wise men who thirst for the fruit of knowledge. They live with H.I.M. and have attended school higher than any college. Wisdom does not come to fools as it only comes to men who have enough common sense, to go look for it. He who is waiting for his doorbell to ring will not acquire anything good from God.

You shall not receive what the kings of the Lord shall receive, for being of the lazy breed of Cain's blood seed, which possesses the internal darkness/ignorance of Mother Eve's/Earths undisciplined children.

There is no lot of inheritance for him in thy kingdom of heaven, as he has been cut off from thy royal seed of kings with spiritual-mental wealth. I shall also take the minds key to thy house/church with M3, and he will not be able to see a thing.

Children, I will say to tie, twist, and turn all projects, and things that you inspire to do into the 1/the lord for his purpose.

You shall see how the Lord takes what have done for him, and makes it seen by everyone who is watching from his kingdom.

Do not look to Israel the place on earth for the resurrection of the Lord's kingdom. Israel are the nation of enlightened people, who shall stand with M3, the head at the top.

I know that many of thy truths have let a lot of lost slow people down to be lower than they already were.

However, the word of truth has also lifted many heads up from low suicidal, detrimental demons of the mind. It has lifted those who were already aware of M3, higher spiritually-mentally into extensive ample thought.

Kingly Thinking resorts to months, and years of unconflicted meditation.

As the incoming messenger with the Lord's messages must settle in the mind-3ye to manifest the spiritual light.

Step into thy captivating spiritual-mental kingdom away from the captive stagnate state of the dark mind-3ye, that the serpent-government and its blood demons have you drowning in.

The slave minds speak of what the serpent-government will do as they do nothing to change its course. I call these weak men, the pirates who jump ship that wreck smooth sails. Surely, they will ride your ship, and do nothing to upkeep it. It will be the blessing of the Lord if you make it back ashore in one piece.

The starship has arrived and has made a roll call of its passengers, as all are mentally ready for takeoff. The Lord always knows what he is doing as he is time and patient in his virtuous acts of victory. In this act of calculated patience, he shall be victorious in getting you to see.

Life has already been preserved for he who drowns not in the soil of sin, where the wicked seeds of killer weeds from hell dwell. The truth has been revealed of Anu-Anew, being M3. A New day-star of enlightening light, and the giver of life. The fiery planet-Sun that cometh, and shall Passover.

You see, there are many reasons to not believe everything that you read. The serpent-government has its wicked hands-servants in everything, deceiving all that your minds-3yes perceive to be real.

Men become Crowned/Christened/Anointed with the spirit/mental wisdom of the lord. Enter thy kingdom of metaphysical kings, where you shall sit up high in heaven with M3, as the wicked lye below, as dust at the bottom of thy holy feet.

METAPHYSICAL

MATHEMATICS

Flaming Chariot/Spirit

Captains log, the Mega star-Sun ship has landed and deposited flaming chariots/spirits/stars to beam you children up to M3. As this is the flame of the mind-3ye in he, who is on fire spiritually-mentally and is ready for warship.

This chariot-spirit has descended to bring up kings-jewels of gold unto the house/church/body of the Lord. It is not an automobile, or any kind of car but instead an anatomical transmuting, transcending transportation.

This is the reward for the mind-3ye being lifted into a new lighting, enlightening abundance. Children do not be blinded by the history that is given to you from the hands of those who want your royal places on earth. That would not make much sense. Would it?

There are no space ships, as there are only stars which are within thy children of worship. The spirit-mental is the only atomic flame with enough reflecting octane to reach the high places of a new. This spirit is not low, and slow it gives the mind-3ye an atomic spiritual-mental boost into clarity.

Let the wicked see those who ride with thy cherubim in spirit/chariot, he is real as Elijah for him to be able to receive this sporty kind of transport from the father/future-Lord.

Surely, it is nice, pristine and shines in the 3yes-minds of men who have witnessed its speeding movement.

It is sweepingly swift as the winds when elevating the minds-3yes of these men into a new alien-X-Unknown dimension.

It is a spiritual-mental time machine with no wheels, but only metaphysical wings-hands. It moves at the speed of light and takes overnight storage in hosting men with the minds/3yes of righteousness.

It is a light mobile which parks itself within dark-ignorant men. Start your engines, as I shall ignite you with enlightening light/spark. Therefore, you may continue to move forward into history with the rest of the real kings from the future.

You shall ride the wave of immortality with M3, in the comfort of thy flaming spirit/chariot, as you shall not hear, or see evil from in here. Just relax on cruise control, and allow the chariot/spirit to do the spiritual/mental steering. As thy chariot/spirit is always fed up, on fire, and ready to ride out to the enemy.

I can never forget what thy enemy has done to thy father, who has given M3 many spirits/mentals/stars. Admittedly, it is those men lifted by thy spirit/chariot who shall be taken to himself, where no one can see him.

He must now allow the commands in the chariot/spirit to speak its data to him when no one is there to distract him in the middle of the incoming message. I tell you that those who do not have a chariot/spirit in their mind's storage will try their dimmest to make you crash with your own.

He who incidentally crashes thy chariot/spirit also falls spiritually-mentally. The chariot/spirit moves fast but also knows when to slow itself down, as it adapts to is hosting drivers head, hands, and feet. The chariot/spirit has lasers of truth, and when actively in deep space of thought, puts on its atomic boosters. It takes off into metaphysical flight.

He who is within the chariot/spirit is traveling in spiritual-mental overdrive, while the slow/low wicked are still sitting on pause at the green light.

He, with the light speed has peeled out and sped off in his racing chariot/spirit. You cannot see him, as he is too far gone ahead of you blind people. He is of the invisibly, invincible when he is flying high with time-the lord in his flaming chariot/spirit/mental.

He is moving faster than a speeding bullet, for he is a heat speaking missile with an atomic dragon bomb that blows light-fire in the faces of his coward adversaries.

He blows away their lies, and plans by dropping new clear word bombs of sweeping atomic light-enlightenment, which exposes their wicked sinister hands to the world.

The flaming mental-spirit/chariot hold more active heat and lightened energy than that of any dark mind, which has a cold interior. When you enter the comfort of thy warm, spacious, chariot/spirit, all lights of enlightenment in the dashing headlamps/stars automatically shine on. There is no other designed ride, into thy spiritual-mental place.

He who has no chariot/spirit is stranded in a no man's land, where all the men are ignorant and all the same, congesting the fast lanes so that the flying stars cannot pass by them. Look at he who falsely claims that he does so much with his time/mind watching M3, he can see that I move fiercely, as I switch lanes in thy chariot/spirit.

Thy chariot/spirit hands have not the calculated time/mind to wait on any man, as he has no time/mind for cowards with their passive female game playing. He hustles to the stars with no limit in his mind/3ye, he cannot see anything besides lightened open space, as he chases none other the father/future.

He remains immortal, even as he has passed through hell among many immoral, mortal men who have tried to change him.

However, all that he can manage to see in his envisioning mind-3ye is to be the best G star that he can be.

Therefore, he has stood firm as the first, and last king/man who has not taken oath, vow, bowed or joined hands with any earthy organization, mosque, church, or synagogue.

He stands alone with the power, and source of all things as the father lives far away, but ye is close to him. The slow men in low groups keep their eyes-minds focused on you because you reap alone, what a group of lost fools cannot recoup.

The wicked ignorant want to compete with the wise men. However, the unwise will need a time machine, to catch up to them as they are in another galaxy with stars/kings/4ths.

The wicked hate him because he stays in a lane of his own, alone away from them. As he needs the hand of no weak man to become great, as he will do all with the lord. The gangs and groups have recruited many fatherless/godless weaklings who are pretending to have their hands full. However, instead, they are busy watching you, real men, stand on your own two feet.

Surely, the wicked only seek to tarnish, mark up, and break chariots/spirits. They are envious of you men of realness, as they are unwilling to pay the cost that is due to be real and TRU. The higher up the lord raises you sons/stars above the slow/low. It will be easier for the wicked to be able to see your chariot/spirit shining among the stars. They will then come running, as if they already knew you, and were your helping servants-hands.

The cowards want to climb inside of your exotic riding chariot/spirit, as they want to bring it down, and destroy it.

However, they cannot get in, as you are on your way up to the Lord's house without them. Allow M3 to identify the UFO's (Unidentified Flying Objects) for you people.

They are merely the serpents-governments remote-controlled drones, as there is nothing above among the stars, other than all that is natural, and TRU.

The many alien abductions, are stories of dark lies that the elite use to mentally-spiritually own you. Just as they bring forth many false dark witnesses to bear lies against you, in their dark courtrooms.

The wicked know that you sons/stars are working to bring down Babylon. Therefore, in everything that you pursue, the serpent-government will be working against you. They will hate, and look to employ other gangs of haters to form against you. The wicked do not like you, because the Lord-Father has taken his time/mind with you, and made you special.

They know that you were not made, or taught by man but instead genetically born a genius to win. You were sent by M3, to teach and enlighten them. However, no one ignorant-dumb wants to learn what is TRU, which they will need in the future that comes from the tongue of he who they already hate.

However, this is why he has the lord's enlightening chariot/spirit with him and, those of dark hatred do not?

What will you men remember when you reach the top if the pulling gravity were not trying to pull your chariot/spirit back down to the bottom?

Faith is the fuel for thy chariot/spirit, as he who worries not works/worships because he has fiery faith, that he shall prosper and prevail.

Children, I tell you to use the mind/9 in meditation and think hard on the evil things that the serpent-government has done to you, and your elders. Such things which have cooperated, and taken a hand in your current situation of slaving subjugation.

TRU kings/jewels/4ths come from the bottom, not the privileged elite, as he loses everything in order to gain all.

The wicked rotten rich spread their riches and lies, unto the even more wicked rich.

The worst fear and nightmare of the governed-mentals is knowing that whatever possessions that they have been given from the Vatican below. Once taken, they will never get back again, as it does not come from the limitless spirit-mental above.

Children, learn where to find thy chariots/spirits which are commuting among you, as they are not cars or space shuttles. They are spirit mentals which are on fire with the truth as those who are in chariot/spirit are in enlightened flight, within the deep dark space of the mind/9.

They have risen from the worthless dead into the living purpose of the lord's proof. Their father has sent a ride to pick them up and bring them back home.

Remember that thy scripture is spiritual/mental, as he who reads literally, deceives his own mind-3ye away from being able to see metaphysically. Thy word has ended many debates, among wise men with sensible, practical reason who read it.

The unhappy, and unwise roam about looking for nothing good, as they have failed higher learning. They are broke, and cannot afford thy chariot/spirit, which requires their minds/3yes attention. Those men with inferior dark minds have no chariot/spirit of fire burning aflame within them.

They will never possess, or own anything this priceless as they're doing the worthless immoral things that they do. While hiding their faces, and hands behind their lying excuses.

The lions/kings/4ths have come out of Judah to be carried back up by thy spirit-mental/chariot, which shall travel where no mortal man can go. It swirls up into the air, to a place that many have never before seen. I come to he who has fulfilled thy promise, it is thy gift-present unto he who has reached M3-the future, in his mind/3ye.

The spirit-chariot has come to bring all that is right up unto its greatness/the lord.

As it never shakes or breaks down on the roadside. It knows thy road well and has a job to uplift thy leaning broken signs-stars which have been defaced of thy word.

He who passes by in his chariot/spirit is glad because he knows where he is coming from, and where he is going. You cannot keep him held behind you, with your nonsense. He is smiling, as only he knows what gold thy chariot/spirit of the future, holds inside for him. He has had many spacious vehicles. However, he has traded them all in, for thy flaming time machine.

There is nothing that can compare, as the richest men with sense would offer him every car in their garages and all that he has stored in the bank for thy chariot-spirit. Have you not known? He with thy priceless chariot/spirit knows that he can obtain all carnal things, which is he the reason that he will not sell, or barter thy chariot/spirit to the hand of any wanting man.

He shall give it to him, as he has obtained it from M3. He shall eat and drank of the word and be changed. Thy chariot/spirit of fiery light descends to pick up he who has looked to become alien to all that which is of ignorance/darkness.

I say that he who gains access to thy chariot/spirit has gained access to many chariots/spirits. He has become a king of the 9/stars/kings, as he has come through M3(The SUN).

Let the wicked who promote the darkness/ignorance of the Vatican live their false sense of earthly security. All while the righteous live in the spiritual/mental way of the levitating mind/9. The chariot/spirit minds/3yes fly high like eagles, as they see all of the snakes and rats crawling in the grass. Ye shall clamp down on their necks, with his flesh tearing talons.

Children your world/road is infested with snakes, and rats.

Nevertheless, thy chariots/spirits with drive shall fly right bypassing the old, unto a new road/world, leaving the ignorant behind in the rear-view dust. Waste none of your precious time/mind of faith on fools, as his job is let you down every time that he is to do something good for you.

I tell you that there is nothing that you can do for those slow/low people who do not want to change. You must turn your back, get into your chariot/spirit to pull away from them and keep on going forward into your minds traveling destination/destiny.

Their sense of time/father/the lord has not come to the false sensing, sinners of darkness. However, your time/father/lord has come for you men to stand up, and become TRU stars with H.I.M.

Become 1 with the chariot/spirit. Feel it, and allow it to feel you, as you adjust to its new improvements, and advanced dynamic performance. Stay focused on your daily progress, like a jewel/kings struggle, and hardships come in the process. Rely on no man, as men will be unbelievable and unreliable to any origin enlightened jewel/kings in this day.

They will sabotage you, in hopes to ruin your plans of affirmative action.

You will not be able to find any men who are good and able to doing anything righteous. They are all after what is liable and available to them right then, which is the soul-minds reason that they are losing.

Do not do what the ignorant wicked are doing, as this is how they get close to you to control what you do. If you are selling vehicles or real estate, the wicked serpent-government will flood those markets with blood, simply to spill their blood claim onto you. Thy panoramic chariot/spirit has clear, unobstructed 360 views so that you are able to see the lurking outsiders, around you that are looking for a way into thy chariot/spirit.

For if you men, are not mindful with attention then the wicked will ransack, and rob thy chariot/spirit of its blessings-gifts.

They will come for the spiritual-mental secrets to what you men alone, are able to do with the time/mind, which has been awarded unto you. This war is between common sense of the enlightened light, and ignorance of evil darkness.

Therefore, I ask. Which overshadows which of the 2 inside of you?

Are you of the ignorant dead, or the awakened wise? The ignorant will say that they are wise. However, the wise are busy showing their wisdom, in what they have been spiritually-mentally chosen to do.

Now, that you have the spiritual/mental word of insight to be able to physically act, and fight. The serpent/government is going coil itself around you, even more than it were before.

It shall terrorize Christ likes, all TRU's believers and real jewels-kings into believing that they have no TRU Lord, who has come to save and raise them from pain.

The serpent-government shall move from doing underhanded deceiving deeds into outright forcing darkness/ignorance upon you logical men. You will see ignorance/darkness being upheld in everything, as though it is TRU light/enlightenment.

Thy word is a TRU delight for M3 to write, as none with a high spirit-mental will dislike, or deny thy truth. None other than those low sinful cowards, of which I already despise with the perfect hatred of eternal demise.

They shall receive thy eternal blade of the sword-word, in thy TRU hope that it cuts internally deep to the soul's core, past the flesh-meat. Therefore, ye shall reborn to breathe again, and begin to speak, and bleed the truth for M3-the Lord.

Truth is with the light/enlightenment of consciousness, as it in the minds-3yes of those with thy flaming spirit/chariot.

For he who is without light-enlightenment in the mind-3ye, has no conscious truth of thy spirit/chariot within him.

It is being written, a man without thy wisdom of truth will only lie to you, as he has not any enlightening reason not to. The righteous lightened image is everything, and money is a mere tool for he who already knows this worth and power. However, worthless, weak men will do anything to earn a dollar and false image.

They will put on uniforms and costumes without having any particular knowledge of the field that they display. They will go around in disguise, pretending to be wise, destroying the lives of those who don't know what to look for to expose them.

The wicked said that they had fiery chariots/spirits because many of you blind children had no clue as to what thy chariots/spirits were. However, in this day thy chariots/spirits of flame that have come to uplift are indeed with, and in you.

Listen not, to the lies of lazy, thieving men who do nothing, as the lame weeds of the mind-3ye linger in every dry field, in this day acting as though they are the hardest working. When instead, they are killing everything of good natural growth in sight. Chariots/spirits are for kings/jewels/4ths, not for the thieves of these kings, who have tried to steal sealed valuable contents from thy precious chariots/spirits for their own use.

Hopefully, within these 3 books in 1, which thy chariot/spirit has brought 4th, you shall find plenty of the blessed word to take from M3 to use for himself, and bless-pass over unto someone else. The geniuses have had the Lords spiritual/mental genes in us from the time of the genesis/beginning, as we are academically, biochemically, and physically different but gifted in that approach.

The ghostwriters, speakers, and teachers for the lord-universe must now activate their flaming chariots/spirits, as it is now time to ride for your justice.

I have added the fuel of faith to your burning souls/minds desires, as thy aligned chariot/spirit of atomic flame request to fly low, and travel into your mind-time zone.

As the captain of a chariot/spirit fleet, 1 must make judgments sensibly with navigating, discretionary direction, and sound detection, to lead thy fleet over the lightened horizon into TRU glory.

6th Element is Spirit/Mental

When water, fire, air, and earth combine together as 1, they form the 5th element of man, who then with the 6th element spirit of the Lord is whole, and complete/360. Without this vital elemental, he is a shell of a man just as many of you have become without any spiritual/mental substance. You are already dead because you cannot think yourselves out of a wet paper bag, which already has holes in it.

You have fallen to the darkness/ignorance of much matter where the elements of light/enlightenment are dim or do not exist. This has happened because you have been broken of the way of the natural elements.

Therefore, you are spiritually/mentally lost in the affairs of the dark world. 56 is the man who is with spiritual-metal of common-3 sense-6, that walks with M3, the 3 elements.

He is with the water of winter/the father, the sun of summer, and thy spirit of the spring atom air in his lungs. He is a TRU element-mental king/4th, and wherever he walketh, or whatever he chooses to do with his hands, there will be no man before, or after him to come, or come again.

These spiritually mantled elemental stars are the Lords/Universes best-kept secret. They are the truth speakers, and seekers of those righteous men who are willing to fish with them, among the dark waters-masses.

Surely, they are the dark water as they are still the Lord's people. All of them, the ignorant-fools, and the enlightened-intelligent.

This is a day for spiritual-mental enlightenment/light so that the pure elements are exposed to those in the painful process of becoming jewels/kings/4ths.

He who becomes 1 with the elements, spiritually/mentally becomes 1 with the lord. Surely, in the process of becoming a man, one must learn to stand up on his own feet.

In the birth of a child water is the first stage of life, then as he exits the womb, he is transferred into the light, whether his eyes are open to its shining or not. He breathes fresh air/spirit, at the same time that he is exposed to thy light-enlightenment.

He is a born-again spirit/mental. Do you children not seek to be born again like him?

The 6th element is spirit/mental, and is the Lords, as it is the element of gold that he has cometh for. Not water, fire, air, or land. Instead, the man with all 6 in he, who has metaphysically, and alchemistically mastered all of the elements in one leveled mind/3ye/time.

He who has the element mental/spirit of the Lord will not follow the church which has murdered and molested children. He is wise of the time-lord and takes an oath with no man.

Thy elements/spirits shall speak for themselves, as time/the lord has scheduled a mandate to express his faith, and show face. His confidence-faith is as water, his fire is the truth, and his will is with the spirit-air that ye breathes.

He is thy flesh king with thy mental-spirit star crown with him, as the Lord is crowned with M3, the 3 360's-Suns.

He is a Priestly 3rd with M3, which transfigures him into a 1 3rd aka a King/4th, who sees with the Levitical levitating 3ye-Mind/Sun of His Majesty/The Lord.

I tell you, that what a man does with his mind/time defines him. For, if he pretends to be wealthy when he awakes all will be gone.

However, if he works to become wise, then he shall be wealthy on all of his walks in life. As he is already awakened to his designated purpose, which brings abundance.

Any man without thy 6th elemental sense is not complete in his mind, as he is half of a man, just as any traitor, coward or sodomite.

This is a mind view of what spiritually/mentally weakened men with no 6th element sense falls into the nonsense of becoming. As they are easily misled, just as small children, and dark/ignorant women.

It is the Lord who makes men into stars/kings/4ths, it is he who illuminates them for the world to be able to see, his TRU glory working from within them. The Lord is Great as his light is magnificent, he brings men out of their troubled paths of darkness/ignorance with his exposing lighting magnificence.

I can tell you, people, many things. However, I have only come to say what is relevant to you and your future/father. There is no relevance is chakras, yoga, and Kundalini teachings. The holder of the 7 churches/chakras is M3 and no other. All of these ritualistic, idol things may help your body become healthier. However, it alters your mind away from the transcending truth.

Do you believe that the strong spirit-mental of the Lord, will abandon a man because of some of the sweets that he eats? Or would it be the things that he thinks?

The spirit is a mental source which means, that it is operative of the cooperative minds/souls of righteous thinking men, that will not adhere to eating anything that someone hands to them.

The wicked world has given you lies to climb, as lower false stagnate stages. While the wicked elite wage fights for their way into thy kingdom, without having to pay M3 thy daily respect of spiritual-mental acknowledgment.

You cannot exile the lord from the written law of spiritual/mental transcendence. He is the bearer of the spiritual-mental/6th element.

The wicked have made you children lose relevant focus on becoming more spiritually-mentally intelligent. Into falling for everything, which is of demonic ignorance/darkness. They have ushered you into welcoming, embracing, accepting, and tolerating their nonsense.

I say to you people that the 6th/Lords spirit/mental element is not prevalent among you. However, it is commonly seen among the spiritually/mentally motivated minds-3yes of real kings. Many of you men have fallen to become that of what you once morally and utterly hated.

You know that you have taken a fall, and now you have resorted into manipulating the way that thy dark people spiritually/mentally view you. As they are blind, and unable see you, and your kind for the weakened cowards without 6th/spirit/mental/the Lord that you are.

A conditioned mind will bring the unconditioned body of a man a long way, away from those men in which the Lord hates, and shall pour on destruction.

It is in the inquiring acquisition of 6th elemental wisdom that a man's DNA in blood transforms.

He is no longer the same as you ignorant/dark average people, as his exceptional mind and blood is not the same as yours. He is wiser and willing to grind harder than you are to become an elemental jewel/king/star. This is what is in the DNA, of he with the activated spirit/mental of the Lord.

He separates mere mortal men from the Lords elemental Kings/Jewels/4ths, with the spiritual/mental intellect in which he brings 4th.

The Vatican/Satan can have the fools of darkness/ignorance; however, the lord shall only gather those stars/men/kings with his enlightening spiritual-mental intellect.

The 6th element is the God spirit/mental of full awakening consciousness, as he who has not this element of consciousness is dead/ignorant. The wicked have labored you people into mining material gold for them.

However, the Lord seeks fishers of spiritually golden men who shall gather in more of thy metaphysical spirits/mentals/gold.

You children have been enslaved by the ignorant/dark carnal demons of hatred, that are unable to deliver you thy spiritual/mental word of good news, signs, or clues.

Surely, playful boys will be playful boys until they become wise men. As a fool shall remain as a fool until he learns to adopt wisdom in mind. For that which is of importance to a man's mind/soul, he will come to take from you.

If his soul/mind desires money and gold, then he will want your money, and gold to be his own. If his soul/mind desires and request for thy wisdom, then ye will receive it. As thy wisdom shall become of his own wisdom if he remembers to keep it with him. With, and in 6 days/stars, the Lord has given 6 pure elements unto the world.

As each day/star/church/hand, had taken part in his overall plan.

Let, the 6th element of spirit/mental common sense in, as the Lords element of light/enlightenment shall come into you to shine along with it. They are 1 in he who is 1 with them in mental/spirit, as he who is 1, is 1 with M3. The Lord who is crown of the 3yes-minds elements, in spirit elemental 3rds/Priest.

Human beings are spirit/mental beings which give an enlightened hue. While the mindless monsters of the dead are those who have tried to change you, men, into beings of ignorance/darkness, which possess less spiritual-mental human wisdom than even them.

The wicked of nonsense cannot wear you real men's spiritual/mental, crowns of common sense.

However, they sport your children and women as though they are their own. The wicked believe that watching you enlightened men with thy 6th element, even without learning anything will help them advance ahead of you.

However, they are wrong, and way behind time/the lord of relevance. Graceful is the grateful 6th elemental king with thy blessing of the supernatural, levitating/Levitical spirit/mental.

He has looked past the foolishness, as he has passed through the Death Valley of the foolish in the world.

He has even tried giving them thy word of spiritual/mental advancement. Nevertheless, the wicked have refused thy word of truth, and thy messenger that cometh along with it. 6 stars/days bring 4th 1 complete day/star.

This can be observed when looking upon the Seal of King David. As ye shall see, the root spirit elemental crown of David, and the 3ye of the Lord.

Thy Sanctuary/Church body is a hallowed, sacred elemental place. As 6 elements/churches form thy 1 Holy elemental Church/Sanctuary/body, from among thy sorted elemental people/jewels/kings.

Thy word cometh with thy 1 Sun, and 4th/King of Judah, who carries thy 6 spiritual-mental elements with him, unto thy Choir/Xmen/10th.

Have you children not listened to those kings who have sung in song subliminal message in psalms unto you?

He who allows his art to be the elemental expression of what his heart desires is a spiritually/mentally revolutionized weapon of atomic fire. As his 6th element of spirit/mental has been sparked with enlightenment by thy Sun/3ye of fire. He has trodden out of the dark waters, into transitioning light.

Let the eyes of the wicked spies to watch as thy spirit elementals transfigure into enlightening/lighting gold that is blinding to those people, with bad stigmatized stagnate minds/3yes.

The way of thy spirit/6th elemental man is through water, fire, air, and earth land, and again he shall go through water/the lord, fire/the sun, and air/spirit all in order to be allowed elementally into thy symphony.

3/spirit, 6/sense is the seal of thy elemental wisdom in the minds/3yes of men. Darkness gives a reason for him to shed his light on its matter. For without darkness, the light would not be the saving day/star that he is. What would he pull you confused, children, away from, with his lighting wisdom?

I tell you that there is a timed seasoning for all things to happen, as time is the reason for all which has already happened and shall reoccur in the future.

The Lord is all, he is light, and the darkness. The past, present, and the future, the day, and the night.

He is the 4 seasons of winter, summer, spring, and fall. He is addition, division, subtraction, and multiplicity. Have thy not revealed the face, and signs of the Lord unto you who see the 1 in the 3, and M3 in the 1?

He who is a king/4th is with 6th spirit element, as he is of the 10th, as a 6th in a king-4thof the 10th. Say, blessings to all men who comprehend as the future/father has spoken the word, which seals the minds in the most real of his kingly men.

These kings/4ths with the processing 3ye/minds possessing the 6th element of gold belongs to H.I.M. Not the earth/mother, not any women, or men, not governments, churches, or organizations but the Lord/Universe only.

This is the TRU Mans day to rule over the 9, with the 10 within him. As the 6th element of celestial ancestral priests/3rds and jeweled kings/4ths are among you. Have thy not told you that a priest/3rd is a king/4th, as a king/4th is a priest/3rd?

This is so, as you cannot become a King/4th before you become a priest/3rd. You cannot get to the blessings of a king-4th, without first coming through M3.

You must come unto 7 with M3, to be of thy 10th magnitude of magnificent stars in comely choir, as the 3 360 Suns in 7 are the 10-X.

The kings-4ths with the Levitical 3rds/priestly, spirit/6th are thy 10th choir of lighting mass, and I AM their Christ-Anointed Head & Crown.

Look deep into the numerical repetition of thy spiritually structured scripture.

I AM the wise counting, countering clock who returns/revolves to put to rest the theories of wicked doctrines, demons, and their scientist.

You children must have a strong mental/spirit within you, so that your mind/3ye does not go astray when seeing, and hearing these many evil things in the world. Man is not alone a physical body, but also a metaphysical leveled, elemental being. What this means is that man is not supposed to literally wonder where he has come from, as this is the wandering worrying mind/3ye of Satan.

All that Man/Adam must know in this particular instance is that he has come from the Lords 6th elements of spirit/mental, and it is through spirit elemental vision that he shall return unto Atom/the Sun.

Where did the first of any living thing come from?

Why do you mortals look to be responsible for everything, even life itself? No one can give you anything good. It has to already be yours, or you have to take it away from those who possess it.

Surely, I see where this is going, as I have given the math of the future/father to you children. For, if you are coupled as 1 unit with thy spirit element/6th. Then the 7 Suns/the Lord-God is with, and in you. I have come up from the nothingness/darkness of the spiritual slums.

Therefore, I had no one to go to for refuge other than the Lord of light, who giveth life. 36's elemental is through levitating, meditating the mind/3ye, that ye shall find M3/M1cha3l/The Head with, and in the 6th *Father/Spirit Body/Sanctuary.*

The stars of high velocity are grounded from dark gravitational pulling forces, as they cannot be sucked into the ignorance which gratifies the masses. His spirit/mental is stable and solid/real as the elements of water, fire, and air on earth.

He is wise, and in his time spent alone has come to realize that without the 3ye/mind of the Lord, that he would not have the elemental wisdom, which holds the key to a good life.

The low thinking fools will wonder how you elemental men have done what you have done to get far away from them. As they know nothing that would be of much spiritual/mental value to you men. In this day, the wisest men shall remain standing alone, all while doing much with their time/mind.

Many men, women, and all of their friends have become the slow/low swine to Rome. People hate what they cannot control, as they will do anything to control its destination. He who is focused on his goals of gold in his life has no time to waste watching what someone, who does nothing is doing.

However, the wicked elementally dead/blind men that linger around doing nothing are watching you elemental men with much intrigue, envy, and hatred for being 1 of a kind with the unable to copy wisdom, which comes from your mind-3ye.

This is TRU wisdom that you must live in realness, to be able to receive and give. The wicked do not live in spiritual/mental righteousness, neither are they real within to be competent in the mind to be able give word such as this to you men, and it is known.

Transfigure your minds configuration to become of thy golden spiritual/mental, intellectual element stars. I have seen your reality. Now take the time, and use your mind-3ye to connect to M3, so that you are able to see into mine.

I shall mine/gather gold from the minds of those men that I have fished into thy kingdom. I shall then come to reap the sons of men, that have morally taught to stay far away from the suffocating hands/servants, and merchants of Babylon/America, and Rome.

The dark/ignorant unconscious minds are filled with Marches/Earths madness. While the minds/3yes of the righteous are filled with thy spirit/elemental of lustrous gold.

The spirits of the Lord's elders are with you children in this new 7th day of spiritual/elemental enlightening,

He is the 1st and, last day for you to be weak because you do not possess thy spirit/elemental, which brings 4th's emancipating wisdom. The Lord was the beginning when men were full of darkness.

It shall be the end of darkness/ignorance when, these men become full of his enlightening-light giving sight, and are no longer frightened of what was to come out of the darkness, as they cometh from the light.

In the light, you men will know that you are in the right place. You shall see men/jewels/kings of all ages, and nations with the same word of truth in their timeless 3ye/minds, and thy radiant smiles shining on their fixed/focused forward faces as they refuse to look behind.

Ra's Elements are an Alchemist best friend. As they are pure, rare specimens of the spirit/mentals mutation of metals.

They bring together in bonding the continuous, robust and never-ending flow of conscious water, with fires determination, and spirits/mentals occupying light into a preoccupation.

I give this TRU word as evidence, and proofs of thy elemental/spiritual existence, within thy natural/raw elements, and the mentality/spirituality within you real men.

If ye are in darkness/ignorance, then the Lord will have a body/church full of lies.

However, if you children are in light/enlightened, then a body/church full of truth will shine bright, with M3 at the top. All that is factual has actually taken place in mind-time/the lord.

For it has his factual/actual math, which stands firm behind holding it up above all lies that seek to become it, and/or beat it down.

At the end of the days/stars word, the truth shall always prove to be victorious. He shall reign above in glory, for all to see H.I.M. unchanged in history/his-story.

Truth is with the spirit/elemental of holy men, as they are thy anointed/Christ kings. However, Satan's society places the wicked slow/low ignorant/dark above them because of their spiritual/elemental advantages. They possess the 3rds/Suns sight, and the Lords/6th sense. They see dead people, as they sense their ignorance/darkness.

Therefore, the dead people want to rid the world, of the intellectual bred sons of thy mentally/spiritually mentored men.

They were once weak, and in darkness, however, the Lord has made them strong, by giving them the magnesium energy that comes from inner light movement. Surely, spiritual/elemental data processes at the high speed of inner bright movement/enlightenment.

For as soon a one breathes thy wisdom, ye who receives the information/data within can then act outwardly on new knowledge.

The wicked can run. However, they cannot hide, or run very far because wherever they shall go, the future/father will be standing in front of them waiting with his 9/Levites/stars. The deceivers will never go around, or manipulate Time/The Lord, no matter how much they try in their darkness/ignorance.

Get down with the real G M3, or stay down below in hells darkness/ignorance. Where the spiritually/mentally unwell dwell in much chaos, and turmoil.

Those men possessing thy 6th elemental sense are constantly on the grind, to shine as the rare jewels/kings that they are. They are always on a pursuit to become better men and to not fall where men before him have fallen weak to the way of the sea beast.

I tell you children in detail that he who uses his own dark/ignorant mind/3ye to connect with M3, and mine of the levitating 9 is 1 in 7 with the 33/Lord/6.

He has put together an effective, healing remedy to come up here with M3. As it through M3 that 1 receives a priest/3rds wisdom to become a 6th/spirit, elemental King/4th. Follow M3, as I move swiftly when in course. I AM no superhero I AM supernatural. I AM what is factual/actual and relevant in its revealing mind/3ye.

I AM Time, the King of Ages. The king who had once walked with a ghetto full of enlightened Nazarene/Stars/Kings of blood, draping over thy dark body. The hand of no man could come against M3, the Christ/Crowned/Anointed, Jewel/King which giveth metaphysical, and physical powers to thy other born jewels/kings/stars of thy bodies-churches.

For those who shall live with M3 as of now. Shall also live with M3, later in thy house away from this world.

However, it is only through the living spirit/mental that one is able to get unto the blessed life afterlife. He shall be able to do this process of elemental, chemical bonding many times thereafter. The Lord of Lords, is the head of the houses/churches, as he has not come to lead you children into more darkness/ignorance.

Instead of into the light, where the truth resides rightfully at home by his side.

1 3rd + 3rd in M3, is a king/4th of the levitating 9/mind. As the Lord goes by many names, therefore in his storybook of life, he goes by the first, and not the last.

It is the first of a man's given name by the father, which holds thy elemental prophecies meaning of truth, and the spiritual-mental metaphorical proof of his life's given lightened purpose.

He who gives truth shall always give a piece of something great to you special people, which comes from his good sound, god/6 spirit sense of golden, elemental, consciousness.

His life is a time/mind consuming grind, as ye consumes natural elements to lift up his mind-3ye, into spirit/6 elemental kingly/jeweled consciousness.

He consciously hustles his muscles with thy spirit/mental. Therefore, ye shall sell all in the world, other than his soul/mind/3ye. Which houses thy 6th spirit/elemental, naturally resourceful, common sense which problem solves, gives, and retrieves all the Lords blessings.

The Shining/Enlightened 1's

The Shining/Enlightened 1's have returned with their leading Star to harvest their genetic gold/spirits that are in those of you men who have chosen wisely to receive it.

He has cometh in this brightened day to retrieve, and receive all who are shining/enlightened, spiritually/mentally in the minds/3yes possessing the truth. These are the bright stars/sons of the Lord who Israel, as they are aware of many worlds, are wise with many words, and shining with enlightenment on many dark/ignorant matters.

Why would thy shining 1's/sons/stars be of ignorance/darkness, when they are indeed full of light/enlightenment?

These stars are anointed with thy crown of spiritual/mental common sense, as they are expedited in their exposure of truth unto those of false pretense. He is the lord's son with a dome filled with exclusive, executive wisdom.

These are the shining/enlightened stars which bring 4th thy word of Anew/Anu day. They have come to tell you the truth of the fallen, that have been depicted as kings.

All that is anew is of the Lord/7th day, there are no such space ships only thy flaming shining/enlightened spirits/chariots/1's. The darkness/ignorance has taken over, where thy shining/enlightening-light once existed, this is the shining/enlightening, inspection of the minds/3yes in jewels/kings.

Thy illuminating enlightened kings/stars/1', shine extra bright with their internal wares of the lightened, spiritual/mental fixture.

Thy shining/enlightened 1's shall join in a light choir, at the top of the Lord's house in Zion, where thy Israel/bodies of stars become 1 with thy head in Jerusalem.

This word is not for the dead, whose time has not come yet for them to awaken to a new reality. They are dull of light, and not yet shining/enlightened with the wisdom of M3/Common Sense.

All of the men who claim to be of thy wisdom have gone down into the valleys where the wicked murder the innocent so that they can lay in their graves with dead women. These are the bottom breeders of the ignorant/darkness, as they are not nearly spiritually-mentally advanced like the sons/stars of Atom's-the Lords shining Atomic light/enlightenment.

No, Indeed. These dim lits are not the human beings of righteous shining light/enlightenment. They parlay and think of nothing fruitful with the days/stars given shining-enlightenment. Let us men stand, and walk among you in the steps of thy shining/enlightened ancestors, as we've come saddled with their ancient futuristic wisdom.

Why believe that the fallen were Gods? For, if the fallen were Gods, then why did they fall?

I tell you that there is 1 Lord above all Lords, that are with and in his spiritual/mental images which shall never fall. Not even, while he leads by exemplifying example. He shall have the light/enlightenment to stand tall, in the eye of darkness. In the hour of the mass, shining/lighting/enlightening.

The dark, ignorant talk with such sophisticated whits. However, they do what the unwise do with their mind/time. Which they could be using, to gain more shine/enlightenment.

Are you still wondering who are the shining 1's? I say that the brightest of the shining-enlightened, inner lighting kings/jewels is the head (Spirit) of the class of classic kings/men/stars.

Surely, without the 1st kings/jewels radiance of shining/enlightenment, those other jewels/kings would be in darkness, confused, with no direction.

It has been a long time waiting, for you people even though it has only been days for M3. I have delivered you, when exposing the shining -enlightening wisdom for you, to give yourselves unto M3.

He shall not aim his sling to kill 2 birds with one stone. Instead, he shall aim from high with his wise, mind/3ye to drop fiery shining/enlightening stars, onto the heads of the beast of Babylon. The shining/enlightened 1's are living proof of what you mortals/dead men, must advance to become in real truth. As they are thy watching minds-3yes, and writing hands/-servants.

They are the intellectual founders of your culture, as it is known. The shining metaphysical spiritual-mental giants of EL(Brightness), brought 4th the resources, and the sources intelligence in literary word, math, and all of your extracurricular acts, and activities.

The shining 1's give the light-enlightenment of substantial solid elemental substance to all subconscious beings, that are submerged in the still, stagnate waters/peoples of darkness.

There are not many subjects that they do not have light/enlightenment to shine onto. He is wise with his band of rays, in an array of ideologies. Children, do not worship the shining 1's/stars, as they are not gods.

They are thy servant priest, kings, and messaging stars who carry thy light-enlightening covenant.

Great wise men shall pass thy lineage of shining light/enlightenment unto their sons, who shall also rule with a wise priest head, in their kingly fathers' stead. His profound high knowledge shall keep him above dark water, and far ahead of the mortal-dead men who raise wicked hands against him.

I tell you that the Anew/Anu hybrid race of shining spiritual-mental giants have been born again, with and in you people. They have now been called up to ascend, until the subsequent time of thy 2nd coming judgment.

Thy shining/enlightened 1's attribute to you people is thy wealth of spirit/gold. This inheritance of intelligence never becomes spoiled or rotten in its way. It will not lose it compositing, composure, and become bad inside its mind/3ye. Such as the yield, which has spiritually-mentally decomposed into ignorance/darkness. He is the will, the way, and the shining/light/enlightenment, belonging to the Star-Lord of the North, in this silent hour of the night.

Shining/enlightened 1's. I will tell you that it is your time to rule. Do not fall into allowing the wicked to overshadow you with antagonizing lies, which come from their dark hypnotized minds/3yes. The foolish will speak in tongues unto you without any truth, eternal meaning, or reason in their words. As though they are, the chosen Christ/Anointed/Crowned 1's.

These sensitive, synthetic men are cynics and will do anything wicked, to shift your minds/3yes direction away from your spiritual/mental gold/goals, that they see you pursuing for the Lord. The dark/ignorant, wicked want all that cometh of you shining/enlightened 1's.

However, indeed, the most essential element that the wicked come for is your soul-mind, which produces-host, spirit/mental, shining-enlightening gold.

Admittedly, I could also tell you, children, a lie/myth. Then go out into the desert to plant, and find thy own false archeological remnants of the Annunaki. However, I have told you much more truth, of the TRU Shining-Enlightened 1's. In which the world has labeled-branded in your minds/3yes, as the same extraterrestrial entity.

Have you not known that the TRU Face of the North, is the face of the Lord-Sun?

I have witnessed many mortal fools lingering around M3 so that they can see what is in thy mind/3ye. Nevertheless, since it has been revealed in this day, you now know what thy shining/enlightened mind/3ye is seeking. It seeks a special unique blended mental/spiritual mixture, which has produced, multiple gold producing jewels/kings.

This is truly history/his-story being created by the prepping shining/enlightening, hands/servants/stars of the Lord.

I AM the historical Arch, crowned logical of the Lord. Therefore, I find nothing logical about the archaeology done by the hands of wicked men who want rulership.

How foolish with ignorance/darkness would I be, if I were to take anything from those who have already stolen everything from M3, and thy own kings?

The shining/enlightened 1's, spiritually/mentally meditate as their forefathers, who were wise before them. While the ignorant/dark pestilence of nonsense, covered the earth taking over the minds/3yes of fallen men by the generation.

These men had not yet become fully wise-awakened with shine/enlightenment in the mind/3ye, to be spiritually/mentally be seen, and received by the Lord/Universe as, kings-jewels-the shining-enlightened 1's.

Why do the dark/ignorant claim to see shining remnants of thy father in M3, then claim that thy same traits of spirit/mental gold belong to them when they have raised M3 up with nothing enlightening?

I reveal to you that the lies and laws of the wicked land will become darker/ignorant along with its internally dark people. However, it will be frightening for those of you who are not aware of the change that is coming. Many men will lose their riches, and along with these worthless items, will go their minds/3yes/souls sighted focus/attention on spiritual/mental development.

Resulting in a suicidal entry into genocide, as they step onto the dark side onto deaths path to be slaughtered, and cooked alive in hell's kitchen.

The Lord is beaming up to new life, those shining/enlightened 1's as he is the 1st levitating Levitical/priestly, Sun/Spirit-Mental to emerge last, from the low slums. He is the chosen 1 who has come to free the decided 1's, by igniting and amplifying their illuminating shining-enlightenment.

You said that you wanted to see astronauts. Well, here they are. The Alpha/leading, shining-enlightening 1's/stars with, and in the Omega/last day/star. Label us whatever you like. The Sons of Atom, The Shining/Enlightened 1's, Angels, Anunnaki, Stars, or thy Suns/sons of man.

Nevertheless, you are the realest, shining/enlightened 1's/figures, in the flesh that will show you the levels, and how to metaphysically scale them.

The emerging stars of the Apocalypse shall show you, children, how to climb up thy spiritual/mental ladder into thy minds/3yes heavenly place.

Where those extraordinary figures manifested in thy kings-jewels, link up like chains in the choiring, inquiring, and acquiring spirit/mental.

Thy shining/enlightened 1's have not come to Marches/Earth to be chained or to chain and force you dark/ignorant people into more of the slave labors that you have already being led into.

These stars descend to deliver the fathers futures day/1000 years of eternity unto those neglected, oppressed Hebrew/black men, and all men that cometh after them. The serpent has given a month of worship to its worshiping/working women, as the Lord shall provide access unto all the days/stars, to those spiritual/men with his future plan of common sense.

The ancestral figs/stars have cometh down from the tree of life where their root-spirit/mental shines above, as the dull, flaky leaves have fallen to the ground to die.

The roots are those men who's minds/3yes are focused on M3, and the dead are the ignorant dry falling minds/3yes that cannot see, which shall become scattered about by the wind shortly.

The time will rapidly come after when many of these falling minds/3yes shall be rounded up, and burned with thy truth. As those who have accepted the word shall be lifted up on thy metaphysical wings, to fly as spiritual/mental eagles.

Do I not have a strange/mysterious way of revealing things?

On the receiving end of thy revealing word is the mind/3ye of a wise man, who has been reading not only the Bible seeking M3 but also the days/stars/signs of TRU prophecy.

The shining/enlightened 1's are not the drinkers of wine or strong fermented drink.

As this may cause a congesting demonic blockage in their conscious, logical, priestly crown's/minds/3yes, critical, crucial thinking.

Surely, if you seek to become a shining/enlightened 1, there are some things that you are unable to ingest.

Wine with evil spirits and parasitic swine intestines are at the top of that not eat, or drink list as these are delicatessens to the Romans.

The shining/enlightened 1's shall leave their marks on Marches/Earth, as a result of embarking on their spiritual/mental journey.

These beings shall leave you people the new word, math's, geometries, and all sorts of alchemy, and academic studies for your minds/3yes to make feast upon, in due time.

Surely, if your mind/3ye is wise in its comparative, comprehension. Then you shall see the overall picture, and not a contradiction. As there are leveled scales being placed into position of the new balanced mind/3ye, where they were missing.

Open your souls/minds, and let the shining/enlightened 1's in to take their places. Wherever the liberal shining/enlightened 1's visit, there is no concurring, conquering darkness with, or in it.

The shining 1's had once fallen. However, now is the day for them to spiritually/mentally rise up to return to M3. The Brightest Shining/Enlightening, 1/Sun/Star of them all has come for those stars who have been stuck in hell on earth/Marches.

He shall return you jewels-kings unto the future/father, so that you are ready to return to Marches/Earth once again with H.I.M to stand as judges, in thy next seasons reaping, and judgment.

Time/The Lord shall return, to relieve the world from its viral distress of wickedness, as there is nothing that you children shall not prepared for when the future-father comes.

Every person has a different journey on their path in becoming a shining/enlightened 1. However, the same applied principals and truths are needed to reach their spiritual/mental gold/goals.

Moral truths and principals shall bring you together in 1 common purpose, which is designed revolving around 1 Spirit-Mental mind/3ye/Sun.

The 1 people are the Lords/1's bodies-churches. Therefore, holy people-churches become enriched with thy spiritual/mental gold, as thy shining/enlightened 1's. This will lead you to be free, into a spiritual/mental land where you can conquer, and obtain any and everything that you focus the powers of your mind/3ye on.

The shining/enlightened1's shall defeat darkness/ignorance with wisdom. When, and wherever this infection of the minds, stem decides to rear its head. The shining/enlightened 1's are the eternally living, all while the wicked are the spiritually/mentally dead.

Indeed, the shining/enlightened 1's, 3rds which have fallen, had fallen when they had taken an oath with the dead/ignorant.

The ignorant-dark who have led then in turning their minds/3yes away from the Lord.

However, they can now look upward again, away from the poverty of ignorance/darkness, denial, and shame and step into this new day of spiritual/mental cleansing.

Shining/Enlightened 1's, it is time for you to reunite with M3 in thy spiritual/mental dynasty.

Leave from M3, since you now have thy word, speed, and wings to fly above which allows every ear, and mind/3ye see the power of those shining/enlightened 1's who have descended from planets of fire. You are the TRU shining/enlightened descendants of thy spiritual/mental 6th element, with thy inclined brightness in their dark mind's storage container.

However, in order for you children to receive the hidden contents of inheritance which belongs to you.

You must first give your minds/3yes acknowledging, attention in spiritual-mental payment unto the Lord.

It is as you receive thy golden spirit/mental that you shall also receive shining/enlightening from he who challenges Rome, and it's wicked for his birthright to rule, the TRU New world.

I AM a TRU descendant of King David from thy spirit/mental lineage and blood. I wear the descending crown of the priestly shining/enlightened 1. The wisdom which poured into King David's shining/enlightening Psalms, as the many written Proverbs, and composed words, and works from producing prodigal kings/jewels. Cometh from the Lord, who handeth his word to these shining/enlightened 1's.

Enlightenment, Wisdom, and Knowledge are as the past, present, and the future. An enlightened soul/mind will grasp for wisdom and in this enlightening wisdom. He shall gain the necessary knowledge needed, and as he begins to know ye will also remember his objective, and will never forget his purpose.

You see, first you children must be able to listen, and read carefully.

Then your soul/mind will have obtained just enough of enlightenment from a shining-enlightened 1, to want to seek more wisdom.

In the process of earning intellectual wisdom, through gaining enlightenment that you will observingly grab hold of many unknown things, that shall give you a learned professors perspective knowledge.

Do not spend the focused attention of your mind/3ye, wondering how you are going to die. Instead, focus your minds/3yes on how you are going to live for eternity with M3, in the future.

The dark/ignorant can believe whatever they want of M3. What sense will come from their beliefs? However, thee still holds the key, decree, fate, and 1 TRU faith of all humanity. In the mandated ordered decree, thy princely shining/enlightened offspring shall re crown themselves as thy spiritual/mental kings.

It was from heaven to earth they came, and now the time has cometh to spiritually/mentally return home above. Unto a TRU heavenly space, prepared by the hands of the Lord to suit the shining/enlightened 1's.

Rise & Shine

I commanded you men to rise & shine. This is your spiritual/mental instruction to raise your minds/3yes from your dark affairs, and come forward into enlightening intelligence, so that you may shine. You see, in the spiritual trans union, you must transfigure, by configuring and confirming new spirit data, and only then comes the transformation.

It is on this alchemistic, metaphysical level that you have become 1 in mental transfiguration, to experience a total transcending spiritual/mental, place/space of transformation. It is in the transformation that 1 transcends, as it in the transcendence that the transfiguring mind/3ye is able to transform.

I tell you again, that the law of the Lord is in the moral order, as all things have a beginning and an end. Light rains from above onto darkness, as spirits/mentals reign with thy enlightenment above darkness/ignorance.

TRU spiritual/mental individuals are the intellectuals of the world, they have the common sense to rise to the occasion in standing for something great. The teacher calls them up to the head of the star class, to share their enlightening/shining brightness with the rest of the students who are in the darkness of failure.

If what a man does with his time-mind, does not make history, then it is no real hustle that shall generate anything good. How can you people be pleased with your current condition of forgetful living?

He who has the spirit wants more than what the hands of pagans from other nations throw to him.

He is a man/king/jewel by all means who shall rise, and shine as ye shall walk away from his paraplegic mind.

It is now that time for the spirit/mentals in the minds/3yes of rare men to rise and come forward to take changing, charge in spiritual/mental war with M3. These men are mandated to speak, write, and teach the truth of the Lord, and to bless those who receive these words in their own moral certainty.

For, that which rises also comes into shining light-enlightenment, as it shall rise above the ignorance of darkness, which bounds many souls/minds to be trapped below in a manipulated hell.

Hell is metaphysical, as it is both spiritual and physical, as the body goes wherever the mind takes you. Your world has gone into the way that the pushing leaders force your minds/3yes into. If you evolve into hell, then it is because your leaders are slowly dragging you down.

However, time/the Lord's plan is still in full revolving motion and movement.

Hell is a cell of tormenting, stagnate sub-consciousness-reality for the human soul/mind. As a cell fashioned of metal, and stone is a tomb for human flesh, and bones. In these levels of hell, you have those that toil in spiritual/mental torment, as they are the dead which are still living.

Therefore, a cell in a high-level security prison of hell is where his flesh, and bones may come to dwell because his mind/soul has already been lowered, into a conventional cell of spiritual/mental limitation. Long before he actually arrived into the physical, place of being in hell alive.

That which begins in the physical must be finished in the next life of pure consciousness. It is determined by you, while you are living where your mind/3ye will be carried away to when your flesh dies. What do you think the Lord is readying you people for?

If there were nothing more, after this life of the flesh. Then ye would not prepare and welcome you unto death, and into the life of a conscious spirit-mental found thereafter.

He who rises, and opens up his Christ-crowned-anointed mind/3ye has come a long way from a path of destructive darkness/ignorance. Into a new day of light in spiritual/mental thinking and deliverance.

Hell is where your minds/3yes will be if you do not look to see M3, the 1 who has the key to free you in his word. Rising is an elemental process of pureness, which requires the wisdom from common sense, and courage to know that what the father/future holds for you, is there waiting to be claimed.

When a wise man is in a land of fools, he will rise to the top because the foolish do not know what it is that the wise man knows in spirit/mental. In which he uses to advance unto the next metaphysical level.

This is the advantage of the awakened-wise, who have risen from the dust of being behind to shine with their intellectual, and physical strengths.

Let the losing weak loaving ends of men with no sense, continue doing what is dark-ignorant to keep up with the fast, flying, and more intelligent, advanced men, so that they may win the race.

Those wicked slow/low heathens have placed blame on the men with strength for their shortcomings, and weaknesses because he is moving fast, with thy strong spiritual/mental gift of Christ/crowned/anointed intelligence.

The wicked dark/ignorant have murdered all that is real and intelligent. As I AM the first and last of the bright shining 1's of revealing relevance. There are less than a few of you good, intellectual men who will be leaving this spiritual/mental life of hell with M3, into a life of eternal integrity.

This is the beginning of a thousand-year period, of the spiritual/mental genetic growth for 10 next sprouting, genesis generations.

They shall be shaped and molded as ripened fruit from the tree of life.

Ye shall blossom in a new season of rising yield, as the Sun/spirit shines his light/enlightenment on those fruits in the field.

Get off of your knee's weaklings, and stand upright like a man, and do something that will earn you some real respect from the world above, those few slow/low people that you now know. Upgrading can be deadly when it comes to many other things if you don't already have a spirit-mental upgrade.

The world has consumed you, into upgrading all that is of material that your darks/minds perceive to be of its worth. You have upgraded your car, your home, and your cell phone. However, you have yet to unplug your minds/3yes to upgrade into a 6th-dimensional spirit/mental.

When all of your physical efforts are gone, and your muscles cannot take anymore weathering. Who will continue to purchase you these lavish things?

What will you birth of fruitful, historical value for the Lord, in order to acquire riches and all in abundance?

I tell you, children, to choose your chariots wisely, as 1 is scheduled to rise and ride into heaven.

While many others are riding, on the road below into hell. Wherever the mind/3ye tells the maneuvering driving host that it is going, will be the direction in which the driver-host will turn the steering wheel to head into.

However, the minds of thy conscious, concentrating, courageous men shall rise up from the puppet stages, and strings of the wicked to come 4th unto the kingly-jewels metaphysical levels. Many of you men have fallen because you have allowed the wicked to penetrate your minds armor with spiritual/mental darkness/ignorance.

You have said unto yourselves, that "The wicked seem to be getting away with everything that they doing in darkness-ignorance."

"Why must I continue to do what is righteous, in the sight of the Lord?" "If there were a God, I would not have to live this way."

However, the truth of the dark matter in your wandering mind is that you would have to live this way, and you do and will until you decide to change/transform.

Whatever it may take to get you, children, to see thy written prophecy, will be unleashed upon you. The dead will wander awake, while the awakened living lights shall be well rested, and restored without worry.

Are you able to see how truth unfolds his revealing hands now?

Raise up your heads away from second class nonsense, if you are conscious that you are no second-class citizen.

However, you are the first-genesis, class of the bright star-geniuses with shining-enlightening spiritual/mental intelligence, which is relevant to the overcoming of the world's darkness.

Wake Up, and meditate on the word, and thy spiritual/mental jewels/kings shall come to you, as they are hidden within the men who carry it with them. Let the ignorant/foolish laugh, as though they are winning. While, all long the mind game that they are playing is to mentally/spiritually manipulate you, TRU jewels/kings into believing that they have already conquered you.

However, when indeed they cannot stop the shine of he who rises with the shining/enlightening truth. He has become tired of being down, broke in the dirt. He has worked many plantation jobs; however, nothing ever seems to come of any of them in his over qualifying mind/3ye. Since the day that he has awakened to a new light, he has not been the same in the mind/3ye.

He now sees his efforts, and reasons for what has been doing with his mind-time with a different light/enlightenment.

Surely, he has spiritually/mentally grown up, as this is what every great father raises his children up under the sun, to have the common sense of his daylight to be able to do.

If you supply and apply wisdom to your children when they are young, even if they do not remember every spoken word, they will remember how you have continuously taught them.

This is the primary spiritual/mental objective, as you must climb into your own mind. If you want to rise and shine above the rest of the broken, and dysfunctional spiritual/mental limbs that could not pass the stress weight pulling test. If you want to win during a time when everyone else has weakened to already give in to the enemy. Then your main strategic elements are within your amplified spiritual/mental strengths.

You shall rise above the skies in the eyes of all the wasteful, promise making, cowards who have done nothing with their lives, besides seek to destroy the lives of other people.

Weak men become emotionally like women when stronger men who already have their way paved out for them do not want to be bothered with his failing, ailing ways.

He who has many sons has seen the weaker of thy sons do hateful, spiteful things to the stronger enlightened/shining 1's for wicked attention. As he was losing, and could not fulfill the same obligations, he then went into a rage as though his mental affliction was the fault of his brothers or any other.

These are the spiritually/mentally weak kinds of men that are your elected politicians, police officers, and world professionals, that bring along with them their inferior, insecure, wickedness into every professional office, and position of power on earth that drastically affects you, innocent people.

Do not be afraid to raise up and chant against what is blocking your view.

No matter how large this obstacle may seem to be, the Lord shall remove it for you.

You have spoken, and written the word in his name; therefore, you have made a vow as his crowned people.

Keep your minds/3yes surrounded with light/enlightenment, as this shall keep the advice of dark/ignorant/evil suggesting spirits/mentals far away. If you plan on taking flight, you must relieve yourself of importing the dead weight that has nothing substantially important, within its stored containment's.

You must drop it behind you, and continue raising up, as you ride into the sun, to no longer be seen by the unclothed/naked, disturbed, 3yes/minds of any man who possesses, not thy spiritual/mental shining-enlightening character of fine lineage/linen. The 7th day/star commands the rising stars of the Apocalypse to shine, with their extraordinary intellectual gifts.

The old pennies of the plantation are historic and rare. Therefore, if you were to find one of them in this day, it would be historically worth more than any monetary gain. I tell you, children, that the Lord has a hand full of these trampled upon men, which have turned out to be golden underneath the surface.

The rising 1's/stars with thy calculated senses have never allowed their minds/3yes to leave their heads, to roam elsewhere. The world is littered with weak men who kill other men, who are more intelligent, wiser, and possess more natural abilities than them. Wise, righteous abiding men, you must hold onto your semen, if you have no desire to give way to this demon, which will come into the world through you.

The wicked of the Vatican are sending out their blood to attack and, murder thy enlightened/shining 1's that have spectacular spiritual-mental hustle. You must know thy rising stars, if you are enlightened with real truth, versus those who are dark/ignorance/evil, hidden among you.

They will soon bring a dark day, unto you ignorant-dark children.

Everyone wicked loves money. However, they do not like those who come from the bottom that has the mind, which needed to survive. Who cares how nice, and cunning these people seem to betray? They are evil/dark, without the rising light/enlightenment of the Lord. He who works for riches and he who works for wisdom are different kinds of men. The enlightened one has submitted, while the other is rebellious because of his ignorance.

Rise above the low-slow souls/minds of the slow-low earth to move faster in a higher spiritual/mental place. For, if you are asleep, it is time to awaken. Whenever the flesh of a star dies from the wicked hands of violence. The serpent/government which hates the Lords spiritual/mental stars has had his perpetrating hands/servants of blood involved to silence them.

There is nothing which happens by coincidental chance, as this would not be possible. It is merely that you do not know the complete story or it's underlying moral. The papacy has taken all of those disadvantaged, weak ends and, missing, lost links. He has made them worship/work for him in dark/ignorant wickedness, for financial strength to compete with the first reborn, who are given a spiritual/mental advantage by the Lord.

The weak ends are the fallen weaklings of men, who complain about everything being too hard for them. If you place him on horseback, he will repeatedly be falling off into the dirt. He will then look around, crying like a girl. As though it is the fault of another that it is difficult, and he has fallen. If you give him the lead, he will still cheat to gain more. There is not light/enlightenment in dark/ignorant people. Therefore, do not look for any 6th sense to be shining there.

They will try holding you movers behind them, even though they are stagnated, stuck on stupid, and are going nowhere.

Allow your wisdom of what you already know, and have accomplished laugh at them, as they are laughing at you men now, they will come to a realizing, halt.

However, when they figure out what you are doing, and how far ahead that you are beyond them. The expression on faces will start changing into disgust and anguish. As they now know what they once did not know of you, and it makes them out to be the little, average ignorant/dark people.

You can only wonder. What has happened to all of the plastic smiles, once your blessed solid works have made the ignorant reality check their own cursed lives? I figure that this is the point where the ignorant began hating the wise men, as they take inventory of the smart sense, then come to notice how much sense that their absent minds/3yes are missing.

You must know that whenever a Hebrew/black man becomes a jewel/king and rises up from the ghetto that he is not as the majority of your governed celebrities.

He must leave from among where demons are roaming about, to head for the exit from their misery, who will soon come for him, and all that he has invested.

Why do you not see people for what they are? This discernment can save you from many troubles, as these demons are passive, emotional, killers. They are the same men who beg you. The same people who seem to be the most docile individuals, as they will cry, however, they will also kill you, out of spite and nothing more.

There are times that a man has to be exposed to darkness/ignorance, so that he may realize how enlightened, and wise that he wants to become. Sometimes he has to be placed around the needy wicked, to see how much more righteous, and wealthier he wants to become. The Lord will take away all of a man's ignorance so that he is grateful to be among the living spirit.

The Lord lowers ignorant/dark men to dark prisons with other ignorant/dark men, so that he is able to talk in private with them. In the hope that they may come to a spiritual/mental realization of how wonderful that it is to be free men, away from the deathly grips of the enemies provoked, provocative sins.

Men are stubborn beings that have to see things, to believe them to be TRU. This is how you have to teach fools. However, wise men have a spiritually/mentally adaptable ability to see instantly where something is going to end.

He does psychoanalysis which carefully evaluates, and examines the minds/3yes of host metaphysically, to logically gain access to its spiritual identity.

This verifying process has never failed in its determining identification in the psychological difference between evil/dark/ignorant, and atomic/light/enlightened spirits/mentals. It is simple that real spiritual/mental men don't have to practice Zen, Yoga, or any other uncharted religious, or spiritual shenanigans.

This is something that is built within you that must be activated by thinking in a new way. You have been enlightened of those blood gangs of Rome with an ill set of different immoral ways. Blue is thy water/people, as red is of Rome, as Rome has sent its blood out to deceive, and destroy you TRU-real believers.

You will know your enemies, by what is on their minds. They will expose themselves with their immorality and misunderstanding of the Lord. Listen to men when they are speaking, and you will hear his moral beliefs, to know whether he is full of nonsense.

There has been an inside war staged against you men, disguised as a truce. As you cannot join into forces with those who have opposite spiritual/mental ways, views, and outlooks than you do. If you do, this will make your enemy seem wiser, and you as the fool who fell, for what the wicked have told you that they will do.

Do you believe the word of wicked ignorant/dark lying people, when they say that they are going to be fair with you?

If so, this would classify you as being a naive, unaware fool of ignorance/darkness too. The sun rises to the top alone, along with his father's plan, without the broken hand, or efforts of any lame man.

He conquers to gain and maintain a position in his story. As the history book of life is the book, which contains the detailed exploits of shining/enlightenment kings.

The wise shall use their experience, and intelligence to rise above the weak cowards of men, who are not good at doing anything worthwhile, besides stealing and lying.

The government/serpent does not go after the weak emotional men, who kill the real motivational 1's. Instead, the serpent/government dispatches them with finances to commit these acts of terrorizing violence. Durable, active spiritual/mental men are rarely worried about anything, unlike the mindless passive coward who is always concerned, and crying about what he is unable to have, and achieve.

The Romans hear his wicked wailing. However, the Lord above all does not see, speak unto, or hear spiritual/mental weaklings. The men of TRU shall stand firm as rising stars. They shall shine on the weak men and their evil heathen women with truth in the spiritual-mental image of TRU.

It is in the contemplation of the dark/ignorant mind/3ye that 1 is able to rise and shine through the hell that he has walked through. It was in the most trying times of his life that he founded the enlightening thought of wisdom, which enabled him to rise and, shine spiritually-mentally as king.

Master Mind/3ye

The spirit mind/3ye is the most potent, powerful biological weapon that you men possess, as he who masters it has also learned and mastered the fight of spiritual/mental warfare. I tell you that a mastermind produces masterpieces of golden composing works. He has a spirit/mental which is out of this world, but also down to earth in carnal host with the master plan.

A mastermind is able to do anything as it has no spiritual/mental limitation within it. It does not back down when it is time for war. He has already seen ultimate future victory in overcoming the vices, and grips of his adversaries. The weak dark/ignorant minds of his enemies do not produce any masterpieces of light/enlightenment. As they have no master or a carefully cultivated plan of action.

A Mastermind is a masterpiece because it manifests the master plan. It opens what is of spiritual/mental origin, and brings it into the dark minds/3yes of the distant destitute man. He is the master who never forgets his spiritual/mental objective.

However, the mind has not changed or slipped and fallen into an evolving enslaved downgrade. Instead, it has transfigured into higher metaphysical levels and realms of spiritual/mental consciousness. I tell you that no one can race or out whit a mastermind as has nothing besides Time/the Lord with him, to be able to come up with these kinds of masterful thesis, and TRU's works of worshipful art.

He is wise in mind with the spirit/mental of the Sun, which places him above all kings/stars/spirits/mentals, as the TRU revealing mastermind of the Universe.

In the magnitude of magnificence is where the great levitating, mind of the master is enlightening/shining in the truth. He is a spirit/mental of strategical, surgical, balance who speaks, writes, and teaches you in metaphorical truth. It is in the word of metaphor that you shall find both sides of the story, and know immediately, which happens to be the truth.

When reading all things, even books, allow the guiding spirit/mental which looks over thy word to work for you to unscramble, divide, and subtract the lies from the truth. The truth is usually right in front of your mind/3yes, even as it is being eclipsed, and buried with dark, filthy lies.

This is when you men must rise, to become kings/jewels with masterminds. Your key is in being able to spiritually/mentally see he who opens the door.

There are no enlightened/light men with mastering minds/3yes, who do not see that all of the ignorant/dark are their enemies. This is the reason which he is watchful and walks into war with the conquering Lord to win, and overcome his battles.

He knows in his mind/3ye that he shall conquer, as the lord has not yet revealed his end time unto him. His enlightening way is as the sun, as his brother is as the moon of blood with an evil star, on his low serpent, serving head.

The mind is an obstacle of dark matter with an enlightening, entertaining pop quiz at the end. Atom's light/enlightenment is the participating, particle in its alternating, spiritual-mental concentrated, acceleration.

Active, ambiguous spirits/mentals of kingly men are restless, ambitious, and relentless in their spiritually-mentally in-divided dual (individual), beings of light/enlightenment.

They have masterminded the wears of spiritual/mental awareness, as they now wear thy priestly Christ/crowned mind/3ye of consciousness and noble linen/lineage.

However, the unaware are naked, exposed, and will be picked apart, piece by piece by the master mind/3ye which sees all. Vigilant, and precise is his insight, as he has given the spiritual/metal lesson which had made the wise raise, to confront and question evil/darkness/ignorance.

The Lord is the spiritual/mental masterminding, mining genesis bank with the ark biology, and DNA dank of all living things. As the mind/3ye of the Universe/Lord has seen all things revolve. He has made men the masterminds of their chosen arts, where no man had the necessary spiritual/mental ability to stand, and star above them.

Babylon/America is a blood gang above the worlds wicked gangs, which has also taken on the faces of many religions, for this is how Babylon/America does much of its silent killing. The weak mind is always available to take the fall; it will be willing to murder the wise men because it turns out to be weak spiritually/mentally.

Kings teach your sons how to master their minds thinking. If yourself neither he, seek not to be historically ruined. The master's spirit/mental is a high sitting Crown/Christ, and therefore, so is the thought that it carries which brings it up above. If he comes up above, then he has proved that he possesses thy master mind potential. However, if he falls below, then this means that he's been robbed of his spiritual/mental Crown/Christening/Anointing.

The mastermind has come to conquer, and take over the many dark/masses of minds/3yes, so that he may lift them into a Christ-anointed, high point in their lives.

Many dark/ignorant men make a claim to be masters of the mind.

However, they are lying, and are covered from head to toe, with their converted wickedness. Look at what groups they are a part of, and what ignorance/nonsense their hands are participating, and partaking in. They have taken oaths, based on the tainted knowledge that the lying givers of these oaths have delivered unto them in ignorance.

Wherever you see the evil star, you will know that it is of the wicked. You shall see it on the Sheriff badge, the Air Force, and all of the star bangle flags. However, these are some of the things that you shall see, which shall identify, and expose your spiritual/mental mortal enemy. This spiritual/mental war has killed the likes of many revolutionaries; however, it has not killed their light/enlightenment, which they have been elected to share with the world.

They have been chosen to do the works of the Lord, who is the master composer of the trained mind, and they are his spiritual instrumentals. Masterminds, it is time to be what you have come down to earth to become as you transition into an enlightening/shining 1. Therefore, you shall see with, in and out of the masters enlightening mind/3ye.

As this is the Christening of a king, who has mastered the chemically balanced minds mental/spiritual alchemy. He has become a master fisherman, and head shepherd of men. He is a master architect and builder of the Lord's church/house. A master mathematician, and the Lord's collecting accountant.

He is the master teacher, and master priest. He is a TRU walking masterpiece of produced art.

A creation designed spiritually/mentally informed, and formed by the mastering mind/3ye, and hands of the Lord, who is the TRUniversal Master, of mentals-spirits indeed.

Suns-Stars
of
Atom-The Universe

The Sun/son of Atom/God is an Atomic indestructible megastructure of light transfiguring enlightenment. He is the head shining 1-star of the shining 1's-stars, he transmutes the new from the old, and the darkened mind into the enlightened spirit-mental for the wise man. I tell you that there is within you star children, as there is in M3 the atomic gold of pure elemental Christ Mind-3ye Alchemy.

Psalm 33

1 Sing joyfully to the Lord, you righteous;
it is fitting for the upright to praise him.
2 Praise the Lord with the harp;
make music to him on the ten-stringed lyre.
3 Sing to him a new song;
play skillfully, and shout for joy.

4 For the word of the Lord is right and true;
he is faithful in all he does.
5 The Lord loves righteousness and justice;
the earth is full of his unfailing love.

6 By the word of the Lord, the heavens were made,
their starry host by the breath of his mouth.
7 He gathers the waters of the sea into jars;
he puts the deep into storehouses.
8 Let all the earth fear the Lord;
let all the people of the world revere him.
9 For he spoke, and it came to be;
he commanded, and it stood firm.

10 The Lord foils the plans of the nations;
he thwarts the purposes of the peoples.
11 But the plans of the Lord stand firm forever,
the purposes of his heart through all generations.

12 Blessed is the nation whose God is the Lord,
the people he chose for his inheritance.
13 From heaven the Lord looks down

and sees all mankind;

14 from his dwelling place he watches
all who live on earth—
15 he who forms the hearts of all,
who considers everything they do.

16 No king is saved by the size of his army;
no warrior escapes by his great strength.
17 A horse is a vain hope for deliverance;
despite all its great strength it cannot save.
18 But the eyes of the Lord are on those who fear him,
on those whose hope is in his unfailing love,
19 to deliver them from death
and keep them alive in famine.

20 We wait in hope for the Lord;
he is our help and our shield.
21 In him our hearts rejoice,
for we trust in his holy name.
22 May your unfailing love be with us, Lord,
even as we put our hope in you.

ABOUT

THE

AUTHORING AUTHORITY

The Author Baba' Tunde Olatacombo A.B. Soremekun is the son of Tauheed Adisa Soremekun, a TRU tribal Yoruba free-born man from Abequta, Nigeria, and a mother who was born a slave to America. Baba' Tunde currently resides in the Baltimore Metropolitan area with some family and friends.

He is an eternal numbered authority of Universal truth within the magnitude and has an experienced over-standing of the journey into the celestial, spiritual realms of knowledge and wisdom through the Suns/Sons enlightening light. "The Earth's youth need the Real Truth," and the author brings it into the mental consciousness.

He is frequently available to speak, teach, and give spiritual enlightenment, advice, and guidance to anyone seeking TRU freedom through the testaments of character in inspiring faith.

His love for the indisputable truth language of the universal order of N.U.M.B.E.R.S. has remained with him throughout his early ages. He is the TRU ghostwriter in the real host who writes numbers into words and words into numbers.

www.7FiGureG360.com

In Zion

In Zion, you shall find M3, as he is thy blazing sun and spirit light of the world on the mountain top. He is always shining in the top of thy mind/3ye through inner lightened and darkened times, as there is no dark day when he is with M3. Zion is a special place for men who think as moral kings; it is the spiritual/mental place where the Lords mind/3ye shall be found.

Surely, as I have told you of Mt. Zion, I have also told you of where the spirit/mental of the Lord lives, as Zion is thy mental mountain above a spiritual Jerusalem. He sits at the top of the dome as thy spirit of gold, which shines its light on thy whole city/church of stars/lights.

For he who approaches the mountain with spiritual/mental belief shall also find relief in its light/enlightenment, as thy spirit/sun in Zion holds the spiritual/mental word of the Lords/Fathers/Futures insight.

INRI

6-10-80 (Seal of ANU/A NEW)

Made in the USA
Columbia, SC
17 September 2019